LOOKING FOR
SQUARE TWO

Millennial Mind Publishing
An imprint of American Book Publishing
P.O. Box 65624
Salt Lake City, UT 84165
www.american-book.com
Printed in the United States of America on acid-free paper.

Looking for Square Two
Designed by Jana Rade, design@american-book.com

Publisher's Note: *American Book Publishing relies on the author's integrity of research and attribution; each statement has not been investigated to determine if it has been accurately made. The author and publisher specifically disclaim any responsibility for any liability, loss, or risk, personal or otherwise, which is incurred as a consequence, directly or indirectly, of the use and application of any of the contents of this book. In such situations where medical, legal, or other professional services may apply, please seek the advice of such professionals directly.*

ISBN Number 1-58982-357-5
Library of Congress Cataloging-in-Publication Data
Mattern, *Douglas.*
Looking for square two : moving from war and organized violence to global community / by *Douglas* Mattern.
     p. cm.
ISBN 1-58982-357-5
1. Peace. 2. Social justice. 3. International relations--Moral and ethical aspects. 4. War--Prevention. 5. Political violence--Prevention. 6. War--Economic aspects. 7. Nuclear nonproliferation. 8. United Nations. I. Title.

JZ5581.M38 2006
303.6'6--dc22

                    2006012581

Special Sales

These books are available at special discounts for bulk purchases. Special editions, including personalized covers, excerpts of existing books, and corporate imprints, can be created in large quantities for special needs. For more information e-mail info@american-book.com

LOOKING FOR SQUARE TWO

Moving from War and Organized Violence to Global Community

by Douglas Mattern

DEDICATION

This book is dedicated to my wife, Noemi—my best critic, best friend, and eternal love.

FOREWORD

We are living in the worst of times and the best of times. The worst of these is that for more than fifty-five years, nuclear weapons have threatened the earth and everyone on it. Testing and production have caused environmental degradation everywhere on the planet and created the possibility of a nuclear war. It is absolutely imperative that we eliminate, eradicate, and forever destroy all nuclear weapons from the face of the earth to keep it the paradise we were given at birth.

The best is the solution offered by Douglas Mattern in *Looking for Square Two—Moving from War and Organized Violence to Global Community*. Since the earth is in peril and the greatest part of humanity is still in misery, we must be audacious, strong, and loving. We must stretch our minds and hearts to the dimension of the problems. As President Roosevelt wrote in his own hand on the day before his death for the speech he was to deliver at the opening of the San Francisco Conference convened to give birth to the United Nations:

"The only limit to our realization of tomorrow will be our doubts of today."

In my view, after fifty-five years of service in the United Nations, this all points to the utmost urgency and absolute necessity for proper Earth Government. It should be number one on the agenda of world affairs at the entry into the third millennium. There not a shadow of a doubt that the present political and economic systems—if systems they are!—are no longer appropriate and will lead to the end of life's evolution on this planet. We must therefore absolutely and urgently look for new ways. The less time we lose, the less nature we will destroy.

I would urge therefore that immediate consideration be given to the proposals offered by Douglas Mattern. It's a matter of life and death.

—Dr. Robert Muller
Former Assistant Secretary General of the
United Nations

PREFACE

Now the trumpet summons us again—not as a call to bear arms, though arms we need—not as a call to battle, though embattled we are—but to bear the burden of a long twilight struggle year in and year out, rejoicing in hope, patient in tribulation—a struggle against the common enemies of man: tyranny, poverty, and war itself.

—President John Kennedy

In this first decade of the new millennium, humanity is confronted with critical problems and, at the same time, boundless opportunities to create a better and safer world. Success depends largely on setting the right priorities for action. As I attempt to show in chapter one, I believe that humanity's top priority should be to rid the world of nuclear weapons, because they pose the greatest overall threat to the entire world community.

Former Secretary of Defense Robert McNamara addressed this issue with his article "Apocalypse Soon" published in

Foreign Affairs magazine. McNamara believes "we are at a critical moment in history." His main concerns are the danger of nuclear weapons, the proliferation of nations possessing these weapons, and the thousands of strategic nuclear warheads that are on hair-trigger alert, ready to launch at just a few minutes' notice.

Another expert working toward nuclear disarmament is General George Lee Butler, the former head of the U.S. Strategic Air Command. General Butler says that there is no security in nuclear weapons and that retaining them is a "fool's game." With the United Nations reporting a total of thirty countries currently capable of producing nuclear weapons, the need for action to stop the escalation and the elimination of these weapons has never been more urgent.

But we must go further. Even without nuclear weapons, modern warfare, with its huge arsenal of indiscriminate and high-tech weapons, is a nightmare of fear and destruction. Waging war for power, conquest, or dispute resolution is no longer an option. The new millennium requires the elimination of the war system itself, with all of its political, economic, and cultural manifestations. In chapter five I will illustrate the profit-based collusion between the arms industry and government and how the war business promotes conflict for enormous economic gain. As detailed in chapter six on the United Nations, future disputes between nations and peoples (and terrorists) must be resolved through the framework of enforceable world law.

Ending organized violence also requires social and economic justice and real democracy. So much of today's violence is the result of brutal poverty and extreme socioeconomic divisions. The bad news is this condition is getting worse, as discussed in chapter eight. This chapter also explores America's gradual loss of democracy to a plutocracy where large corporations and the rich rule. We now have over 225 billionaires in this country and 37 million people living below the poverty line. This is a disgraceful betrayal of the hard-fought struggles for equality by American workers, and it must be rectified.

The first four chapters of this book describe some of the struggles over these issues during the past four decades. While much of the text involves my personal experience, this serves only as an example of what thousands of people have done and are doing today. And the best news is that, for the first time in history, millions of people are speaking out, marching, protesting, and working for peace and a healthy, sustainable environment. This is the life force of the future, because the political leadership in today's world is generally lacking in vision and global perspective, and is therefore incapable of initiating such a huge advance. This is indeed a historic moment: today, the people must lead so that the leaders can follow.

CONTENTS

CHAPTER 1
Last Chance to Make a Buck

If fools and folly rule the world, the end of man in our time may come as a great shock, but it will no longer come as a complete surprise. The warnings given are there.

—UN President Abdul Rahman Pazwak

It was the most dreaded night in October of 1962, at the very height of the Cuban Missile Crisis. The U.S. had issued an ultimatum for the Soviet ships not to pass a designated point, a sort of "line in the sand" on the high seas, and U.S. and Soviet ships were about to confront one another. Rumors and fear were rampant as I rushed home from work to turn on the evening television news for the latest information. The anchorman appeared on schedule, and with an ashen face and trembling voice he said,

"We may be hours away from nuclear war.... More after these commercials."

Yes, commercials, the last chance to make a buck before it was all over. It was then and there that I fully understood the extent of irrationality in this world of genocidal weapons capable of ending the human drama in very short order. Later that night, at the very height of America's collective anxiety that the possibility of nuclear war was very real, the fire alarm siren in our city went off "by accident." I needn't comment further on the effect.

It's often reported that the Cuban Missile Crisis was President Kennedy's "finest hour." Although a great admirer of President Kennedy, I don't believe that this was a great moment for anyone involved. Later information on the confrontation, including transcripts of conversations between the president and his advisors, indicate that the situation was altogether very confused and unpredictable. It was brinksmanship to the limit, and in the end it was Nikita Khrushchev, although guilty for initiating the crisis, who effectively ended it by backing down and ordering the Soviet ships to turn around and sail for home.

I remember the philosopher Bertrand Russell, who had protested so vigorously against nuclear weapons, calling on both Kennedy and Khrushchev to end the absolute lunacy before it was too late. And years later, Secretary of Defense Robert McNamara said we came within a "hairsbreadth" of nuclear war without knowing it, and that "luck" played as much a role as any wisdom.

Earlier that day I gave my first public speech, and having never before made a speech of any kind, I was very shy to do so. The location was Stanford University at an impromptu noon rally against the situation in Cuba. The talk was an informal thing that kept my legs shaking long after my short diatribe was over. My second speech took place the next day in San Francisco's Golden Gate Park where a large rally concerning the crisis had convened. I gave this speech on top of a garbage can attracting what was not an enormous crowd. Nevertheless, it became the first in many years of public speaking on a myriad of peace-related issues.

What was most discouraging about the missile crisis was that it, and the Cold War itself, should never have developed. It seems incomprehensible that the carnage of the two world wars did not produce a dramatic change in human affairs based on ending the mass violence, suffering, and death that marked what is arguably the most violent period in human history. The new age of mass slaughter began with World War I, known as the "War to end all Wars." The spark that initiated this conflict was the assassination of Archduke Franz Ferdinand, who was the heir to the Austro-Hungarian throne. The assassination took place in Sarajevo on June 28, 1914, by a Serbian nationalist. This set in motion a series of events that soon spiraled completely out of control into a global conflict.

For most people, the war was fought for obscure reasons, yet through exaggerated nationalism, crowds cheered as their young men marched off to war. Over 8 million of them never returned. They died in mud-soaked trenches in Europe, prodded on by glory-seeking politicians and generals. A total of 8 million soldiers were killed, and an equal number of civilians were victims as well.

Perhaps the best example of the criminal waste of human life in World War I was the battle of Verdun in France. Raging on for ten months and fought for control of an insignificant six square miles of land, the battle for the trenches produced seven hundred thousand casualties and three hundred thousand dead.

World War I also set the stage for the conflagration of World War II, which produced slaughter on a more massive level as military and political policy targeted civilians as the victims. The absolutely evil Holocaust madness committed by Hitler and Nazi Germany still seems incomprehensible: innocents were murdered, including some 6 million Jews as well as communists, socialists, gypsies, and Russian prisoners of war. The Japanese Imperial Army also committed atrocities that, like the Nazi brutality, were exposed to the world community at the Nuremberg War Crimes Trials.

Barbarism rained down from the sky during this most destructive war in history. Initiated by German aerial bombing of cities like Warsaw, London, and Coventry, it concluded with American and British carpet and fire bombing of cities in Germany and Japan, culminating in the dropping of atomic bombs that instantly laid waste to the cities of Hiroshima and Nagasaki and the lives of over one hundred fifty thousand civilians.

The total number of people killed in the war is still being tabulated, but the figure is estimated at around 60 million. Moreover, some 40 million victims were civilians, a two to one ratio over military personnel. The number of human beings killed by each other is 50 percent higher than the 40 million who died in the 1918–1919 worldwide Influenza Epidemic. It is equivalent to the number of deaths during the Black Death plague of 1348–1351.

During that dark period, humanity was helpless against disease, and the horrific number of people lost their lives as a result. But the slaughter of the twentieth century that continues to this day is self-inflicted. That is why this period of incredible brutality and destruction should have created a dramatic change, in perspective, to forever end such horrendous carnage. That, however, was not the case. Instead, humankind embarked on the creation of even greater destructive weapons. Thanks mainly to the vision and intellect of President Franklin Roosevelt, at least the United Nations was created with the vision of peace and cooperation in mind. However, nationalism remained the dominant force, and the world was soon embroiled in the Cold War.

During the Cold War, over one hundred fifty wars were fought and more than 23 million people were killed, most of them civilians. The moral demise of our civilization is striking when one notes that at the beginning of the twentieth century, 90 percent of war casualties were military and 10 percent civilian. At the end of the century the figures have nearly been reversed.

The Nuclear Age

Whom the Gods would destroy, they first make mad.
—Euripides (480-406 BC)

Surely a visitor from another planet observing our obsession to build weapons of annihilation would believe that the great Greek playwright was correct. At the peak of the Cold War, for example, over seventy thousand nuclear weapons were stockpiled in the world, enough to kill everyone on the planet umpteen times over. And in this fifth year of the new millennium, after all the hope and promise demonstrated around the globe on the first day of the year 2000, there are still over thirty thousand nuclear weapons stockpiled, more than enough to finish off our civilization entirely.

The Hiroshima bomb and its aftereffects killed over one hundred thousand people. But today's hydrogen bombs are so powerful that just one bomb detonated over a large city could kill a million or more people and leave the city in a radioactive ruin that would make aid and rescue efforts virtually impossible.

The International Physicians for the Prevention of Nuclear War reports that a modern 150-kiloton hydrogen bomb could cause somewhere between 736,000 and 8,660,000 deaths, depending on the population of the target city. The superpower arsenals have hydrogen bombs in the megaton range, many times more powerful than a 150-kiloton bomb.

A U.S. Trident submarine carries twenty-four ballistic missiles, each missile capable of carrying eight warheads, each warhead over five times the power of the Hiroshima bomb. One Trident submarine has the destructive power of over one thousand Hiroshimas. There are eighteen Trident submarines, and this is just one component of the U.S. nuclear triad, which also includes ICBMs and heavy bombers. Russia maintains the same nuclear triad, and like the U.S., Russian missiles carry multiple warheads with a single missile capable of carrying the destructive power of hundreds of Hiroshimas.

Moreover, the nuclear danger is rapidly escalating out of control with the nuclear club expanding to at least eight countries, and the International Atomic Energy Agency (IAEA) reporting that another thirty-five to forty countries are capable of building these weapons. Unless this situation is soon resolved, it is only a matter of time before a nuclear exchange takes place somewhere in the world, perhaps spiraling out of control and escalating to a nuclear tsunami that will crash upon us all.

To put a fine point on this most irresponsible condition, a report by BBC found that some scientists and military chiefs are alarmed that a small asteroid passing close to our planet could accidentally trigger a nuclear war if mistaken for a missile strike. No wonder that General George Lee Butler, former head of the U.S. Strategic Air Command, says there is no security in nuclear weapons and that "it's a fool's game." And let's face it—we are the biggest fools of all if we allow this condition to continue toward an inevitable disaster.

Robert McNamara said during the Cuban missile crisis that we came within a hairsbreadth of nuclear war and that luck played a leading role in averting it. Today, in 2006, luck continues to play a major role. Over the years at least twenty close calls to nuclear war have been recorded, and who knows just how many are off the records?

Stan the Man

One of the most dramatic incidents involved a young colonel in the Soviet Army. It was the night of September 26, 1983, with Colonel Stanislav Petrov in charge of two hundred men operating a Russian early-warning bunker just south of Moscow. Petrov's job was monitoring incoming signals from satellites. He reported directly to the Russian early-warning system headquarters that reported to the Soviet leader on the possibility of launching a retaliatory attack.

It's important to note that this was a period of high tension between the U.S. and the Soviet Union. President Reagan had called the Soviets the "Evil Empire," and the Russian military shot down a Korean passenger jet just three weeks prior. Meanwhile, the U.S. and NATO were organizing a military exercise that centered on tactical nuclear weapons in Europe.

In an interview with the English newspaper *Daily Mail*, Colonel Petrov recalls that fateful night when alarms went off and the early-warning computer screens showed a nuclear attack launched by the United States. "I felt as if I'd been punched in my nervous system. There was a huge map of the States with a U.S. base lit up, showing that the missiles had been launched."

For several minutes, Petrov held a phone in one hand and an intercom in the other as alarms continued blaring, red lights blinking, and the computers reporting that U.S. missiles were on their way. In the midst of this horrific chaos and terror, the prospect of the end of civilization itself, Petrov made a historic decision not to alert higher authorities, believing in his gut and hoping with all that is sacred that, contrary to what all the sophisticated equipment was reporting, this alarm was an error.

"I didn't want to make a mistake," Petrov said, "I made a decision and that was it." The *Daily Mail* wrote, "Had Petrov cracked and triggered a response, Soviet missiles would have rained down on U.S. cities. In turn, that would have brought a devastating response from the Pentagon."

As agonizing minutes passed, Petrov's decision proved correct. It was a computer error that signaled a U.S. attack. Petrov said, "In principle, a nuclear war could have broken out. The whole world could have been destroyed."

In our increasingly superficial societies in which celebrity is praised above all else, many legitimate heroes go unnoticed and without reward. Colonel Petrov was dismissed from the Army on a pension that, in succeeding years, would prove nearly worthless.

The *Daily Mail* found Petrov's health nearly destroyed by the terrible stress of the incident. His wife died of cancer, and he lives in a second-floor flat in the small town outside of Moscow. "Once I would have liked to have been given some credit for what I did," said Petrov, "but it is too long ago, and today everything is emotionally burned out inside me. I still have a bitter feeling inside my soul as I remember the way I was treated."

In an interview with Stanislav Petrov on *Dateline NBC* (Nov. 12, 2000) reporter Dennis Murphy said: "I know you don't regard yourself as a hero, Colonel, but, belatedly, on behalf of the people in Washington, New York, Philadelphia, Chicago, thank you for being on duty that night."

At the close of the *Dateline NBC* interview, anchor Stone Phillips said, "Some of you may be wondering just how verifiable this story is. Well, a former CIA official we spoke to told us Russian and other sources confirm it and that he believes it. He says Petrov's account is consistent with what we knew about the Soviet early warning system at the time and the way it was operated. He also notes that the Russian government has never challenged the story."

I learned about Colonel Petrov when researching close calls to nuclear war for an article I was writing for *Humanist Magazine*. I found that Petrov had been interviewed by various media over the years, but that he never received recognition for his action. I felt this injustice must be rectified and decided that our organization, the Association of World Citizens, would present Petrov with a special World Citizen Award. We have presented this award to several outstanding individuals, including Dr. Robert Muller, former United Nations Assistant-Secretary-General, The Reverend Jesse Jackson, and San Francisco mayor Willie Brown Jr.

My initial problem was finding Petrov. We have a branch in St. Petersburg, but it was unsuccessful in locating him. After a few months I wrote a letter to the editor to the *Moscow News* requesting help in finding a former colonel in the Red Army named Stanislav Petrov. After several weeks I received an email from Scott Peterson, the Moscow bureau chief for the *Christian Science Monitor*, stating he had read my letter, and that he found Petrov in a small town outside of Moscow. Mr. Peterson gave me Petrov's address, which I passed on to our branch in Russia. A few weeks later Scott Peterson wrote an article on Petrov that appeared in the *Christian Science Monitor*.

With the welcome help of the *Moscow News* newspaper, we set a date for the award ceremony, which took place on May 21, 2004, at the headquarters of the *Moscow News*. The award was reported extensively by the Associated Press and other media sources and appeared in newspapers and TV broadcasts in the United States, Russia, and some other countries. Finally, after more than twenty years, Colonel Petrov received his long overdue recognition and public exposure for his heroic act.

People reading about Petrov in their local newspapers sent contributions of money to our office to give to the colonel as a tribute for his heroic deed. The donations ranged from a modest $7 given by a thirteen-year-old girl to a couple of $1000 gifts. As of February 2005, over $6000 was contributed to Petrov. In addition, many people sent letters. At Archbishop Carroll High School in Radnor, Pennsylvania, English teacher Thomas Nedelka gave his students an article about Petrov and asked them to write a letter expressing their thoughts. Sixty-five students responded with letters to the colonel expressing their gratitude for his action. Most of the letters were similar to the first two printed below, and some were classic like the last two.

Dear Mr. Petrov: I am writing this letter to tell you my feelings on the event that happened back in 1983. Though I was not alive, I wish I could give you all the praise you deserve. Without your sufficient judgment, the entire United States could have been wiped out. I truly believe that the military picked the most intelligent person for your previous job.

I have never heard of this event until today in class, and I was quite shocked. I never thought that the fate of the world would be unknowingly placed in the hands of one person. This made me realize that some of the most important things in life go unrecognized. I really do believe that you saved the world from a huge downfall and from massive destruction. Thank you for your bravery and devotion; without you, this world wouldn't be the same.

Sincerely, Megan Cromie

Dear Mr. Petrov: I am in the tenth grade in the USA, and I must say that I am very thankful for what you did. I probably would not be here now nor would anybody I care for. Your actions were so courageous that I cannot believe that you do not live in luxury as a prize for what you did. Very few men save the world. In fact, I cannot name anyone other than you. I am writing to thank you for what you did and to tell you that you are a true hero, though I'm sure you have heard that before. I did not know of you until I read an article about your action in my literature class. You prevented a world catastrophe because you were brave.

Sincerely, Michael J. Mercuri

Dear Mr. Petrov: Out of all my comic book heroes, you are my favorite. I was struck when I read the article about you. I thank you for your keen instincts and courageous mind. You should be called Stanislav "The Russian Sensation" Petrov. You should be proud of your name and the lives you have saved. There is no reward great enough for you. You are my hero.

Sincerely, Jonathan D. Gampon

Dear Mr. Petrov: Thanks a ton, man. I love Russia. I basically owe my life to you. If you ever need anything give me a call. I got your back.

Sincerely, Antonio Giovanni Girifalco

The publicity over the Petrov World Citizen Award and exposure of Petrov's dramatic act prompted John Hallam of Friends of the Earth Australia Anti-Nuclear Weapons Campaign to contact me through the Association of World Citizens to seize upon the Petrov story with a project aimed at convincing the U.S. and Russia to remove all nuclear warheads from hair-trigger alert and launch-on-warning before it is forever too late. Forty-four Nobel Laureates, over three hundred organizations and the European Parliament, have endorsed the project. At the time of this writing, the project is reaching the point of presentation to the nuclear powers and the United Nations.

This project is imperative because the four thousand U.S. and Russian strategic nuclear warheads on hair-trigger alert pose the greatest threat to our civilization. A recent study by the RAND think tank reported that the U.S. and Russian warheads on hair-trigger alert could be launched in a few minutes notice, destroying both countries in an hour. Such a doomsday scenario could begin by an accidental missile launch, an early-warning system error, a miscalculation, or intent.

More than a decade after the end of the Cold War, there is no conceivable excuse for this hair-trigger policy and the threat it poses to humankind every day of every week. To continue with this policy is irresponsible, if not criminal.

Here are some other examples of recorded close calls to nuclear war:

1979: A CNN Cold War program reported that a technician at the North American Air Defense Command mistakenly placed a training tape into the main systems at NORAD's Cheyenne Mountain Complex in Colorado. The tape caused NORAD's early-warning system computer to respond that the United States was undergoing a massive Soviet missile attack. NORAD officials were alerted but within minutes the error was discovered, ending the threat of launching U.S. missiles in retaliation. This incident was one of several missile warning system failures that occurred over an eight-month period.

1980: In the August 14, 1983, issue of *Parade* magazine, Jack Anderson reported that on November 19, 1980, two Air Force missile officers were conducting a drill of a simulated missile launch of their Titan missile at McConnell Air Force Base near Wichita, Kansas. When Captain Henry Winsett and First Lieutenant David Mosley turned the keys for the simulated launch, something went wrong. They received a message of "Launch Sequence Go," meaning that the real missile launch sequence was underway. Fortunately, Winsett had the good sense to shut the missile down before it could be launched. Mosley said it couldn't be determined whether the missile's guidance system would have steered the missile to a target in Russia, which would assuredly have resulted in Soviet retaliation. But, he said, it would have gone somewhere "north." This close call still gives him tremors.

1984: As reported on the CNN Cold War program, in August of 1984, a low-ranking officer at Soviet Pacific fleet headquarters in Vladivostok broadcast a war alert to Soviet forces at sea. For thirty minutes, until it was determined that the alert was false, Soviet ship commanders sent back urgent inquiries about the alert as they prepared for combat. In the meantime, U.S. and Japanese forces also went to a higher alert status.

1995: The Center for Defense Information (CDI) and several other reliable sources report that in 1995, the monitors of the Russian Strategic Rocket Force at the Olengrosk early-warning radar site registered the launch of a U.S.-Norwegian research missile probe of the upper atmosphere. To the Russians, the missile's trajectory looked like a U.S. Trident missile that carries multiple nuclear warheads. This set off alarms at the Russian nuclear weapons command, which notified President Boris Yeltsin, who reportedly activated his "nuclear briefcase." For a few minutes perhaps, the fate of the United States—and all of Western civilization—hung on Yeltsin's judgment.

Dr. Bruce Blair, president of the CDI in Washington, D.C. and a former Minuteman Missile Launch Officer reports that both the United States and Russia remain preoccupied with preparing to fight a large-scale nuclear war with each other. U.S. spy planes monitor the Russian coast, and U.S. submarines still trail Russian submarines as soon as they leave port.

As the nuclear crisis escalates with scant reporting by the media, the words of General Douglas McArthur in a speech to the Congress of the Republic of the Philippines on July 5, 1961, are still relevant. "But this very triumph of scientific annihilation—this very success of invention—has destroyed the possibility of war's being a medium for the practical settlement of international differences....Global war has become a Frankenstein monster to destroy both sides. If you lose, you are annihilated. If you win, you stand only to lose. No longer does it possess even the chance of the winner of a duel. It contains now only the germs of double suicide."

And recently in his article "Apocalypse Now" published in the 2005 May/June issue of *Foreign Policy*, former U.S. Secretary of Defense Robert McNamara describes the extreme danger posed by nuclear weapons and general lethargy regarding the reduction of this threat. He writes: "We are at a critical moment in human history," and "We must move promptly toward the elimination—or near elimination—of all nuclear weapons."

McNamara also reminds us: "The average U.S. warhead has a destructive power twenty times that of the Hiroshima bomb. Of the eight thousand active or operational U.S. warheads, two thousand are on hair-trigger alert, ready to be launched on fifteen minutes' warning."

On April 21 in New York, Mikhail Gorbachev criticized the U.S. for its large nuclear arsenal and urged the United States "to cure itself" of hypocrisy over nuclear arms and be prepared to cut its atomic arsenal and take it off "hair-trigger" alert.

Gorbachev said: "I think Russia is ready to cooperate. Now the question is, is the United States—which is the only remaining superpower—is the United States ready to do this? I think not," he added. "[The United States] say other people don't need [nuclear weapons], but what kind of law is this that they are advocating?" Gorbachev asked. "It's the law of the jungle."

Terrorism is a burning problem that the United States must counter. But the greatest terrorism by far is that each day the people of the world continue to be under the threat of nuclear incineration whether by accident or by design.

We cannot count on a Petrov to always be on duty. We can only count on ourselves to have the intelligence and the respect for human life to mobilize with an unyielding determination and apply a constant pressure on the world's governments, particularly the United States.

Martin Luther King Jr. stated the problem precisely: "We must learn to live together as brothers or perish together as fools."

Postscript on Stanislav Petrov:

In December (2005) the producer for the movie on Stanislav Petrov informed me that the director and crew were bringing Mr. Petrov to New York City for ten days to conduct a few interviews for the movie and requested my help.

With the help of Selma Brackman, a dedicated peace activist and president of the War & Peace Foundation, we arranged for Mr. Petrov to speak at the United Nations and to present him with a second World Citizen Award.

This took place on January 19, 2006, in the UN's Dag Hammarskjold Auditorium. Just before Mr. Petrov's talk, I presented him with a World Citizen Trophy made of sculptured glass on a granite base with a single hand holding the earth. The event at the United Nations was filmed for the movie. Other invited speakers for this event included Dr. Bruce Blair (Center for Defense Information), Jonathan Granoff (Global Security Institute), Alice Slater, Rev. Vernon Nichols

(NGO Committee on Disarmament), and Keven Sanders (War & Peace Foundation).

I also arranged a meeting with Walter Cronkite for an interview with Mr. Petrov to be filmed for the movie. This took place the day after the UN meeting on January 20 in Mr. Cronkite's office at the CBS headquarters in Manhattan.

The interview between Walter Cronkite and Stanislav Petrov was an unforgettable scene with the doors closed and the office crowded with the movie crew filming the event, and the conversation between the two men lasting for about twenty uninterputed minutes.

Mr. Petrov was comfortable with Walter Cronkite as the great journalist brought out the full story and drama of what happened on the fateful September night in 1983 when Colonel Petrov took five minutes to make his historic decision, and Mr. Cronkite commented that this was "five minutes that saved the world." I vividly remember Mr. Petrov recalling how he had morally prepared himself for the kind of decision he was forced to make on that fateful night.

We should remember, as the Moscow News *reported, that when Petrov made his decision and called his Kremlin liaison to report the alarm reporting a U.S. attack was false, he did not actually know it was false. It was only after fifteen to twenty agonizing minutes passed, waiting to detect if U.S. missiles were incoming, that Petrov's decision proved correct. There were no incoming missiles. It was a system error that signaled the attack. As the English newspaper,* Daily Mail, *concluded, had Petrov cracked and reported the Soviet Union was under attack, as the warning system was reporting, an exchange of nuclar warheads could have resulted, and as Petrov said: "The whole world could have been destroyed."*

This drama is the focus of the multi-million dollar feature film on Petrov produced by Zentropa/Statement film. The movie is scheduled for release to movie theaters in the U.S. and othe countries around the world in September 2006.

CHAPTER 2
Vietnam—A Lingering Tragedy

When the leaders speak of peace
The common folk know
That war is coming.
When the leaders curse war
The mobilization order is already written out.
—Bertold Brecht

The struggle for nuclear disarmament soon took the back seat to an emerging conflict that proved to be disastrous for the United States. This was the Vietnam War, which should never have begun. It was a betrayal of the people that had fought with the allies against the Japanese in World War II. When the war ended, the French attempted to reinstate their colonial rule over what was known as French Indochina, which included Vietnam, Laos, and Cambodia. Ho Chi Minh, the leader of the Vietnamese independence movement, appealed to Western powers for support, but was rejected. Instead, the United States aided the French with money and supplies. I remember talking to navy flight crews when I was stationed at the U.S. Naval Air Base on Guam back in 1953.

They said that the stop at the air base was to refuel the airplanes before continuing on to South Vietnam carrying supplies for the French.

The French failed in their attempt to regain control over Vietnam. The decisive battle took place at the valley of Dein Bien Phu with fierce fighting that lasted sixty days. When the French realized that they were facing certain defeat, they appealed to the U.S. for direct military intervention. President Eisenhower refused, stating this would be "the wrong war, the wrong time, and the wrong place."

An international conference in Geneva was held in July of 1954 that quickly produced the Geneva Accords, designed to resolve the crisis under the following provisions:

1. The nation of Vietnam was guaranteed its independence.

2. National elections would be held in two years under international supervision.

3. Vietnam would be divided at the seventeenth parallel until the elections, the North being led by Ho Chi Minh. Mainly forces that had fought with the French would control the South. The accords, however, were never put into practice because the U.S. refused to sign the agreement.

The elections designed to unite Vietnam were never held. The South, under the regime of Ngo Dinh Diem, refused to participate because, according to President Eisenhower in his book *Mandate for Change*, "Had elections been held possibly 90 percent of the population would have voted for the communist Ho Chi Minh."

Civil war soon mounted against the repressive Diem regime, which banned political parties, closed newspapers, and alienated the Buddhists. The National Liberation Front, or Viet Cong as the U.S. labeled them, were the South

Vietnamese who began the revolution against the Diem government. It wasn't long before the U.S. determined that the situation was going in the wrong direction. In 1961, President Kennedy responded by sending U.S. "advisors" to aid the Diem government, and by the next year, four thousand American personnel were serving in Vietnam.

This was the beginning of a steady military escalation in support of a secession of South Vietnam governments. Nevertheless, the situation continued to deteriorate, and in 1965, President Johnson sent the first official U.S. combat troops. By 1967, about five hundred thousand American troops were fighting in Vietnam, in what became a full-fledged civil war between North Vietnam, which was aided and supported by the Soviet Union and China, and South Vietnam, which was supported with military aid and troops by the United States and some allies, including Korea and Australia.

This war was host to the most massive amount of bombing in the history of warfare. Before it was over, 8 million tons of bombs were dropped. This was more than three times what the U.S. dropped in all of World War II. The bombing produced over 20 million bomb craters and included such indiscriminate weapons as napalm, phosphorous, and fragmentation bombs, as well as high altitude saturation bombing by giant B-52 bombers. And it was all directed against a small third world country that never even threatened harm to the United States.

Most tragic is that over fifty-eight thousand Americans were killed and three hundred thousand injured, not to mention an estimated 2 million Vietnamese fatalities. The war ended in 1975 with the defeat of South Vietnam and its Western allies by North Vietnam, and it was all for nothing.

The same results would have been achieved by allowing the elections to proceed as designated by the Geneva Accords of 1954.

Protest at Home

As early as 1965 and into 1966, many Americans began to realize the futility and immorality of U.S. involvement in that far away country of Vietnam that most had never even heard of. A vocal, if relatively small, number of people began to protest the war, and Palo Alto, California soon became a center of opposition by non-student, anti-war groups. This was in addition to the notable anti-war activity on the campuses of the University of California in Berkeley and Stanford University.

In Palo Alto, an organization was established called "Concerned Citizens" by people opposed to the war. I soon joined and became the chairperson. This new peace organization was comprised of many remarkable people. I was barely out of my twenties and so impressed that the majority of the group were citizens in their senior years, who had retired from successful careers. Rather than enjoying their retirement, they worked tirelessly to oppose the war and get our soldiers home.

This group included people like Pauline Scott, who had to walk with crutches with considerable pain, but never let that stop her from leading much activity with the organization. Legia Callego was a widow whose husband had been an executive with United Fruit Company in Cuba, and Legia enjoyed sharing her memories of attending grand dinners where the place settings were made of gold and the meals extravagantly sumptuous. But what impressed (or depressed) her most was the extreme poverty of people outside the gates of the huge mansions who were begging for food and help. She was obligated to attend the dinners with her husband, but both sided with the poor against the intolerable injustice, and at the time welcomed the Castro revolution.

Others I recall include Felix Green and his wife, Elena, at their home where we held our initial meetings. Felix Green was an English journalist and the author of *Vietnam Vietnam*, a book that heavily influenced the anti-war movement by exposing the truth about the war. I remember Leo the farmer, an idealistic communist who would have done anything for the cause. He was one of the most selfless people I ever met. Khrushchev's revelation of Stalin's crimes had shaken Leo's belief in a communist utopia, but he never stopped believing that the benefits of labor should go to the workers themselves, rather than to what he considered a parasitic class of money-grabbing investors and corporate executives.

We soon established a peace center in the downtown area that served the entire mid-peninsula about thirty miles south of San Francisco. In the early years of protest, before the "great change" in the attitude of the majority, protesters were a minority and often under attack by those who disagreed. The main activity consisted of small demonstrations and vigils at some symbol of the federal government, often the post office and usually under verbal assault by people passing by. Nevertheless, it was through this type of activity, distributing literature and talking to people, that the antiwar movement began to grow until the majority of Americans opposed the war.

The early years of protest were often marked not only by verbal assaults, but also occasional death threats. I recall a letter written by the right-wing Minuteman organization displaying a logo of a rifle showing a gun sight with a human head in the middle, presumably my own. One or two other people in the area received this letter, demanding a public apology for the cardinal sin of opposing U.S. policy—or else! As I recall, this organization was soon out of business, as they had spent much too much of their time robbing banks.

Of all the threatening letters and telephone calls, the only one I took seriously was a recurrent call from a character who always threatened to come to my home to blow my head off with a shotgun. As these threats escalated, I devised a plan to end them. The next time he called, I quickly cut him off and said that our "guerillas" had traced his phone, knew his address, and if he ever called me again they would "take care" of him. Of course, we had no "guerillas," but he never called again.

One of the events that stick in my mind during this period was a large protest march in Berkeley of about fourteen thousand people that began after a rally on the U.C. campus. The Hells Angels told the press that they would confront the marchers, which was a silly threat that soon evaporated as thousands of people marched by them unscathed. However, thanks to the U.S. media, this motley group of thugs received more news coverage than the protest march itself.

Around this time, our peace center was broken into in the middle of the night, and four very large file cabinets were stolen. The size and weight of the cabinets would have required several people and a truck to complete the job. We lost our mailing and donor lists, along with all correspondence and reference material. The police were called but demonstrated very little interest, though the robbery took place about two blocks from the police station on a well-lit street. Several years later, we learned that the files had been stolen by the FBI in a criminal case that also included files from the Farm Workers Union, which had been founded by Caesar Chavez. I was subpoenaed to the trial to identify and receive our stolen files. But what the court returned to me, out of four large file cabinets, was an 8X10 inch folder with a few meaningless sheets of paper and no explanation of the missing files. Perhaps they are still in the FBI archive.

In 1967, on behalf of the Concerned Citizens organization, I wrote a resolution addressed to President Johnson condemning the use of the barbarous weapon of napalm bombs in Vietnam. I managed to acquire about ten thousand signatures and sent it to the White House and Congress, where it was placed in the Congressional Record, and where it remains as follows:

Congressional Record Archives

4.95. By 1967 some petitions concern the U.S. involvement in Vietnam. The committee received a massive petition titled, "Declaration on Napalm: The Use of Napalm Must Be Stopped!" The petition was printed in newspapers and otherwise circulated throughout the United States in 1967 by a group called "Concerned Citizens" from Palo Alto, CA and thousands of citizens signed the document that declared, "The use of napalm is bringing shame upon our nation throughout the world. Its use is wholly unworthy of the ideals for which this nation stands. We demand that our President and the Members of our Congress take immediate steps to stop the manufacture and use of this barbarous weapon." (90-AS-4, 8 in.)

The Napalm Bomb Plant

One of the major events in our area was the construction of a napalm-bomb-making plant in Redwood City, which was just a few miles from our peace center. The plant was located at the end of a long road that ended at the San Francisco Bay. Because of the desolation of the surrounding landscape, every trip to the napalm plant seemed like a trip to the end of the world.

Several organizations were active in opposing this facility, but it was our organization, Concerned Citizens, that took charge of a constant vigil organized just outside the plant gates. I have many memories of this protest period, as in some ways it encapsulated the protest of the entire war.

Napalm is one of the cruelest weapons ever devised by the mind of man. It is a mixture of gasoline and polystyrene, a type of plastic that creates a jelly-like substance. When dropped from the air, the napalm bomb creates a huge fireball up to five thousand degrees. The napalm sticks to the skin as it burns, and the victim either dies horribly or is brutally maimed.

The actual work of making napalm bombs took place behind a high wire fence that was easy to see through. The plant had thousands of empty elongated metal bombshells stockpiled in open wooden crates. Large trucks transported the shells into the plant, where they were filled with napalm that was mixed in huge tanks at the center of the plant. It was similar to a giant gas station in which the bomb shells were lined up like cars waiting to receive the fuel that was pumped by workers with a hose. In this case, however, it was a fuel that would rain down agonizing, fiery death and mutilation on men, women, and children in jungles and villages seven thousand miles away.

The vigil lasted for several months and usually consisted of one to five people at a time standing with their signs outside the gates, except for special protest days when more people were on hand. The filling of the shells with napalm took place only about forty yards away and was clearly visible from outside, so the employees of the plant were in constant view of the protest.

One morning I was joined by a young Stanford University student. Many students from high schools and universities participated in the vigil. During our conversation, it was clear that he was a very bright young man, but his condition was quite tragic. He was a product of the sad drug culture of the sixties, and it soon became apparent that his rebellion against the war in Vietnam was actually a self-destructive rebellion against his father, a rich man and a leading member of the right-wing John Birch Society. He told me that his father favored bombing Vietnam back to the Stone Age.

Here was such a bright young person, so full of potential and yet destroying himself. I wonder to this day how he turned out. Hopefully well, but it is more likely that he became one of the many casualties of the 1960s culture of rebellion that so often came through our peace center during those difficult years.

A very good-looking woman in her early thirties once joined us in one of the larger vigils. This was one of the days when we were subjected to verbal abuse from people who came to support the work of the plant. In the midst of what soon became a tense situation, the woman started speaking in a placid voice to the hecklers, and we were soon impressed by her demeanor and calm attitude. She never responded to the hecklers with abusive language, but instead said that she felt sorry for them because up to a few years ago she had held the same blind views. On this day she was viewed with a surprising respect by all involved, and this included the hecklers. She truly rose above the crowd, and her presence kept the confrontation from erupting into violence.

On several occasions, we were witness to gutsy demonstrations by Marco the revolutionary. Marco was a tough guy, full of passion. He often attempted to stop the huge trucks from transporting napalm bombs from the plant by lying down at the gate so they could not pass. Marco would remain in that position until he was arrested by the police. More than once, it appeared the truck driver might, in anger or frustration, run him over. But this did not faze the revolutionary. Every time he was hauled off to jail, he sang revolutionary songs and claimed that the day was coming when the war criminals would go to jail rather than those who protested their crimes.

On another day, I was the lone demonstrator for several hours, and a man dressed in a blue suit approached me from the other side of the fence, calling me by my first name. He identified himself as an FBI agent, and in our short conversation, he said he knew more about me than my family did, and that photographs of me and other protesters were all over his office. This was not a big surprise to me, as the FBI regularly took photographs of the demonstrators and recorded our automobile license plates. Nevertheless, it was enlightening to learn this information directly from the source.

One of the most memorable events at the napalm plant involved a member of our Concerned Citizens organization who was a respected psychiatrist in the community. He was a person of courage and moral strength in his opposition to U.S. policy in Vietnam. The good doctor was also a one-man demonstration. Day after day for weeks on end, he would go to the plant with his own truck, complete with signs protesting the war and with his own public speaking system.

His activity consisted of telling the workers through his loudspeaker that their arms were getting tired, and then more tired and weary holding the large hose that was filling the bombshell with napalm. Employing these psychological tricks, he tried to convince the workers that their unconscious sense of morality was causing them to grow exhausted and that their health was jeopardized by this immoral work. This activity may seem silly and ineffectual to anyone not present, but in that monstrous environment, it was a very serious and very courageous protest.

In the end, we never knew if any workers actually quit their jobs due to the doctor's demonstration, because the turnover rate was high for reasons ranging from low pay to poor working conditions. Nevertheless, it was high moral drama and the message was right, but the good doctor paid a heavy price. The publicity from his activity ruined his practice, and he was forced to move to Canada.

Laddie

Now to my dog Laddie, a beautiful tri-colored collie, and my most unforgettable experience in the many months of this vigil. On a cold, moonless, and very clear December night, I was the lone protester for about two hours, roughly from 8 to 10 p.m. I had Laddie with me for company, but it would be the last time I brought Laddie to the napalm plant. We were alone with the guards at the gate and the workers inside methodically filling shell after shell with napalm.

Laddie set upright on his hind legs, which was unusual for the situation and the time involved, as Laddie did not want to play and he was not his usual frisky self. But normality was impossible in the bizarre contradiction all around us. It was nearly Christmastime, and the lights from homes in the nearby hills were shining brightly against a black, starry sky. The sight of people in their homes, warm, content, and oblivious, was a cheery contrast to the nightmare of napalm production only a short distance away. Many Vietnamese men, women, and children exactly like themselves were going to be horribly killed or burned by these very bombs.

Realizing the contradiction, the bright lights in the hills were suddenly not cheerful, not joyful, and not conducive to a happy Christmas scene. It was too sad, too utterly brutal. Looking at Laddie, I noticed that he was shaking and very quiet. The shaking wasn't from the cold, not with his heavy coat. We talked, at least me to him, and he with his eyes. There was no question that Laddie was very uncomfortable and very sad.

I can't explain how, but Laddie sensed from me that this was an evil place. Laddie remained silent, and he didn't stop shaking until we finally left the napalm plant for home. Laddie died over thirty years ago. I still miss and grieve for him, and I will never forget that night at the napalm plant. Laddie, my great canine friend, sensed something was very wrong, if only from me, when so many people in those warm and expensive bright homes in the hills didn't understand or even want to think about it.

Eventually things began to change. More concerned people came to the napalm plant, and thousands were taking to the streets all across the country to protest the war. Within a year, the napalm plant was forced to close due to the pressure. However, this was a bittersweet victory, as the plant relocated to Southern California and continued to make napalm bombs that created the kind of nightmare described below.

One of the most horrific photographs of the entire Vietnam War shows a little girl with her clothes burned off running away with other survivors from of a napalm attack on her village, with the bright flame of napalm in the background. Her name is Kim Phuc, and these are her memories of the attack:

> I remember I was nine years old, just a child. That night we heard the Viet Cong were coming and that they wanted to use the village. And then in the daytime, the soldiers came in and there was fighting.
>
> We were so scared. I remember my family decided to seek refuge in the temple, the pagoda, because we thought it was a holy place. We could seek refuge there, and we could be safe. I did not hear the explosion, but I saw the fire around me.
>
> And suddenly my clothes were burnt off by fire. I saw the fire over my body and especially my arm. I remember at that moment I thought I would be ugly, and not normal like other children.
>
> I was so scared because I did not see anyone around me. Just fire and smoke. I was crying and I was running out of the fire, and the miracle was my feet were not burned. I kept running and running and running. My parents could not get past the fire, so they turned back to the temple and they sheltered there. My aunt and two cousins died. One was three years old and one just nine months—two babies. After that I passed out.

American napalm gave Kim third degree burns over more than half her body, and she later suffered through fourteen months of painful rehabilitation. Even today the scars cause her physical pain, but she says she has found a way to be free of the emotional pain through forgiveness and faith.

It's possible the napalm bomb that injured Kim Phuc and killed her aunt and two cousins was manufactured at the Redwood City plant during the beautiful pacifist's demonstration, or the doctor's psychological tactics, or the night I was with Laddie. Perhaps it was carried out of the plant on one of the trucks that Marco tried to stop. If so, by not ending the plant production sooner that we did, we failed Kim Phuc, as well as other victims of this horrid weapon.

In later years Kim initiated the Kim Phuc Foundation in Canada with the mission to heal the wounds suffered by innocent children and to restore hope and happiness to their lives through medical and psychological assistance. UNESCO named Kim Phuc a Goodwill Ambassador for the Culture of Peace "to spread the message of the need for reconciliation, mutual understanding, dialogue, and negotiation to replace confrontation and violence as a means of settling conflicts."

It's Not Only Immoral, It's Also Illegal

A United Nations convention in 1980 banned the use of napalm on civilians (by any means), on military targets within civilian areas (by air), and on military targets not sufficiently separated from civilian areas (by land). The United States rejected the ban on napalm and continued to use it in Iraq. In March and April of 2004 napalm bombs were dropped near bridges over the Saddam Canal and the Tigris River, south of Baghdad. Colonel James Alles, commander of Marine Air Group 11, said, "We napalmed both those approaches." The colonel commented that "unfortunately there were people there...you could see them in the video. They were Iraqi soldiers. It's no great way to die." In an interview with the *San Diego Union-Tribune*, Marine Corps Maj-Gen Jim Amos also confirmed that napalm was used on several occasions during this war.

A reporter from the *Sydney Morning Herald* witnessed a napalm attack on March 21 at an Iraqi observation post close to the Kuwaiti border. He wrote that "Safwan Jill went up in a huge fireball, and the post was obliterated. 'I pity anyone who is in there,' a Marine sergeant said, 'We told them to surrender.'"

Soon after the napalm plant closed, there was a very large antiwar demonstration at an army induction center in Oakland, just across the bay. This was a wild event that received national coverage, mainly due to the violence that the police used in breaking up the demonstration. A number of people were hurt by police batons, mainly because they couldn't get out of the way as the police charged forward.

My memories of this event center around the induction center and my place of employment, which was the leading semiconductor company in Silicon Valley. Because I took the day off work for the protest, three groups of employees from different departments went to the plant director to demand my dismissal for my anti-American activities, which in those days meant opposing the Vietnam War. Some months earlier the director received a telegram from corporate headquarters to fire me.

Surprisingly, I was not fired, and I continued to work for the company for another two years. But it was not until several years later that I learned why. Another small group of key engineers had told the director in no uncertain terms that they would quit if he fired me. No one in the group was involved in antiwar activities at that time. But they were sympathetic to my cause and understood what was happening. They put their economic well-being on the line. They were good people, and for me, silent heroes.

By 1968, more people were opposing the war and getting involved in peace demonstrations. Our peace center decided to hold a downtown anti-Vietnam march, and we hoped for a crowd of at least five hundred people. To our surprise, five thousand people, according to police estimates, marched down the main street of Palo Alto that day. Afterward, we joined with the protest movement at Stanford University for a teach-in, where I joined with other activists and professors to speak to eight thousand Stanford students. Teach-ins like this around the country were the beginning of a mass movement against the Vietnam War.

While the media consistently focused on a select few protesters, some of them serious, some strange, and some in it for the publicity, it was the involvement of people from every walk of life and every age group that gave the anti-war movement its strength and influence. Hopefully the recorders of history will have more integrity than the media and get the history right.

Soon after the Stanford demonstration, we organized a march and rally right in the heart of Stanford Industrial Park, which included many companies involved in war work. As chairperson of the rally, and with a great deal of publicity, I was very unpopular at work once again and was banned from the R&D building for several years. I soon departed for another company and, over the next twenty-five years, continued work as a senior engineer/manager in the Silicon Valley computer industry, while at the same time continuing full time with my peace work. This was necessary as, while there is an astronomical amount of money and profit in the war business, little or none exists for peace and human rights work—another black mark on the values of our society.

The Packard Affair

Another memorable event involved David Packard, co-founder of Hewlett Packard and the leading industrial icon of Silicon Valley. At the time, he also served as Under-Secretary of Defense during heavy bombing of Vietnam. Packard was to be presented with a Citizen of the Year Award by the Mayor of Palo Alto. This was a big public event in the form of a dinner for the rich and management elite of Silicon Valley.

The peace groups in the area decided to counter the ceremony by giving David Packard a Bomber of the Year Award. The evening of the ceremony, which included a formal dinner, a group of hundreds of protestors formed in front of the resturant. The people attending the dinner, all in their best dress, had to drive through the crowd of shouting demonstrators, so by the time they reached the party they were not in the best of moods. The audience included CEOs and leading executives of the industry, along with their wives, and also, I might add, the director of the company I worked for, who spotted me with some panic at the reception bar.

The peace groups decided that in addition to the outside demonstration, a small group should purchase tickets for a table inside, and I was elected to be the person to disrupt the meeting and ask people to leave in sympathy with the suffering our country was inflicting on the people of Vietnam.

I was at a table with three women, all of them outstanding members of the community and members of our peace organization. We were appropiately dressed for the dinner in formal attire. Also at our table was a group of up-and-coming yuppies who obviously wished to make themselves known to industry leaders. They were soon in for a very unpleasant surprise.

As dinner was served, it became obvious that the FBI in the room had spotted us. The final clue was during the main course, as I was the only person in the restaurant who did not receive a knife with which to cut my steak. No matter how many times I appealed to the waiters, all I got was a lot of spoons.

With the ceremony finally underway, David Packard went to the microphone to receive his Citizen of the Year Award, and I, as planned, also went to the microphone while the other three people at the table attempted to hand out leaflets asking people to leave. Pandemonium broke out immediately. I had never seen such a transformation from polite conversation to vicious name-calling, coming particularly from the women, many of whom wanted to get at my throat.

David Packard, on the other hand, reached out his hand to shake mine. I believe he thought this was some kind of a planned joke. I refused to shake his hand, and at that point, two husky FBI men escorted me out of the restaurant. Now I am 6'2" and weigh about 215 pounds, but I was impressed by their technique, and of course, I offered no resistance. It was a very quick and smooth departure.

The front page of the following day's *Palo Alto Times* newspaper showed Packard and me with Packard's comment "Purveyors of Evil" highlighted in large letters. I felt confident that readers would realize that the only purveying of evil was waging an unjust war in Vietnam. A few years later David Packard spent considerable time attempting to revive the reputation and career of Richard Nixon—quite unsuccessfully, I might add.

Another rather comic situation occurred that night. A very bright and active member of the peace group came in disguise, as she did not want her family name publicized. Her father was a very conservative person and prominent in the Chinese community. Unfortunately, her photograph was on the front page of the newspaper the next day with her family name. So much for the disguise.

Veterans for Peace

Around 1967, I had the honor of establishing a Northern California division of Veterans for Peace with retired U.S. Navy Rear Admiral Arnold True. Admiral True had a brilliant career in the U.S. Navy during World War II and left the Navy at the war's conclusion to become a professor at San Jose State University. The admiral was a wonderful person who was dedicated to creating a better world. He made headlines as a member of the U.S. delegation to South Vietnam to investigate the infamous "tiger cages" in which prisoners of the South Vietnam government were placed under cruel and inhumane conditions. Our best contribution to the anti-war movement as Veterans for Peace was the organization of a peace rally in San Francisco's Civic Center that drew twenty-five thousand people and became one of the largest demonstrations up to that time.

A year or so later, I was invited to a meeting at a home in San Francisco where a Guru from India would be speaking and might provide a large donation to our organization. On arrival, I found about twenty-five people sitting in chairs in a circle around the Guru. I sat in front, and as the meeting began, much to my dismay, the group began to pass around pipes filled with hashish. Now, this was a time when police arrested anyone caught with any kind of dope, and many people were convicted and sentenced to lengthy prison terms. Moreover, it didn't matter if a defendant was totally innocent, as was my case, because of the strictness of the courts. Many people were caught during this irresponsible campaign and sent to prison. So, I was in a hurry to depart the meeting, but I did stay for a short period to listen to the famous Guru, who turned out to be a charlatan. He sat in the middle of the room smoking pot and gulping large amounts of gin, while issuing what the crowd apparently throught were rare metaphysical insights mixed with extreme profanity. Apparently the Guru believed the path to enlightenment was drugs and expletives. I left the meeting with great relief that no police red lights were waiting for me outside.

About 1968, I was invited as a delegate to a large peace meeting in New York City that soon became an unforgettable event. The meeting was held in a large auditorium with some two thousand delegates from various peace organizations. I don't recall the main sponsor, but I do remember that the meeting soon erupted into a full scale riot. The cause was apparently a long-simmering quarrel among competing peace groups in New York, including some very vocal Marxist organizations.

The police were called, but they refused to enter the auditorium as the fighting was rather extensive, some of it near me, as I calmly sat in a business suit watching the action and wondering what it was all about. Finally, some very large union people came from the stage and tossed the instigators out of the auditorium. The meeting then continued as if nothing unusual had happened, and dates and locations were set for the huge anti-war demonstrations across the country that marked the beginning of dramatic change in the attitude of the American people toward the war. Everyone wants meetings to be harmonious, but I've experienced that it's often the chaotic meetings that provide the most important results.

In 1972, we organized another large demonstration in Palo Alto with two thousand people and Dr. Linus Pauling as the featured speaker. Dr. Pauling, a two-time Nobel Laureate in peace and chemistry, made headlines by questioning the mental health of President Richard Nixon. Dr. Pauling and his wife, Ava Helen, also a dedicated peace activist with the Women's International League for Peace and Freedom (WILPF), were often guests of our organization at fundraising dinner parties.

Eventually the war ended in 1975 with a humiliating and reckless departure of American troops and a great unnecessary tragedy for all the American and Vietnamese who lost their lives for the foolish decisions by even more foolish old men in our nation's capital.

The Posse

The war's end may have eased some of the hostility against peace advocates, but not in areas like Dallas, Texas. A couple years later, for example, I was a guest on an evening talk radio show in Dallas. My topic was exposure of the war industry with its obnoxious profits and waste of our vast wealth on the means of destruction and war. The program was two hours long, and the station was inundated with incoming calls, not a single one sympathetic to my comments.

The host of the program said most of the calls were so hostile they could not allow them on the air. But he loved the huge response; so many calls came in that the station could not handle them all. It was all good for ratings. During the

last thirty minutes of the program, a group had formed
outside the station. Like a posse of riders in the Wild West,
cars circled the station. And they were waiting for me.

By good fortune, I had done the show from New Orleans
by telephone and was not in the station at the time of the
program. The program audience, however, believed
otherwise, and the host, taking advantage of the publicity, did
not explain it to them. I learned of the posse from the host
during the commercial breaks. To this day I wonder just what
would have happened to me had I done the program on the
day scheduled.

CHAPTER 3
Citizens' Diplomacy

An invasion of armies can be resisted, but not an idea whose time has come.
—Victor Hugo

Citizen diplomacy is an idea whose time has come. With modern technology, individuals and organizations from diverse parts of the globe can have instant communication through the Internet, telephones, and fax machines. The marvel of telecommunications, along with the relative ease and speed of travel, provide the capability for joint activity among people that was not previously possible.

This has been most significant in the citizen diplomacy programs that reached a high level of urgency during the Cold War as the hostility and antagonism between the governments of the United States and the Soviet Union threatened to plunge the world into a suicidal war. To counter to this hostility, people and organizations traveled to the Soviet Union to meet with regular citizens, and sometimes with government officials, to build better understanding and friendship. As described later in this chapter, Soviet citizens also traveled to the United States for the same purpose and achieved similar results as citizen diplomats.

U.S./Soviet Peace Rally

In 1982, I proposed to the Soviet Peace Committee in Moscow that we should organize a joint U.S./Soviet peace rally. A few months later I received a letter stating that my proposal was accepted and inquired as to how we should proceed. At the time I did not have a definite plan, but by good fortune, totally independent of the peace rally proposal, Howard Frazier, Director of the U.S. peace organization Promoting Enduring Peace, invited me to be a speaker for the 1983 Volga Peace Cruise in the Soviet Union.

I accepted and informed Howard that I had proposed a joint peace rally with the Soviets and that they were waiting for my reply on how to proceed. We then decided it would be logical for the peace rally to be part of the 1983 Volga Peace Cruise, and Howard Frazier traveled to Moscow to finalize the details.

On July 18, 1983, during a sunny Monday afternoon in Moscow, about one thousand Soviet citizens carrying signs and banners stating in Russian "no to the arms race and yes to peace" joined with 146 American citizens from nineteen states to hold the first U.S./USSR demonstration for peace and the elimination of nuclear weapons. With banners held together by both sides, and to the sound of music, the two groups joined in a march through Moscow's Gorky Park.

At the conclusion of the march, a rally was held in the park's large amphitheater where speakers from both sides addressed the crowd. A festive mood ensued with some great entertainment provided by the Soviets, including singers, dancers, and acts from the Moscow Circus. We didn't have any official entertainers on our side, but we did have an amateur harmonica player whose talent was just this side of bearable. Nevertheless, he got up on the large stage and gave his performance, much to the delight of the Soviets, who gave him a rousing ovation.

The peace rally in Gorky Park received extensive media coverage in Soviet newspapers, television, radio, et cetera. As we learned from some tourists we met in the hotel, it was also broadcast on TV in some European capitals. However, it was never reported in the U.S. media, although they had been informed of the event well in advance.

It should be remembered that this was a very volatile time due to the debates on limited nuclear war, President Reagan's "evil empire" rhetoric, and the U.S. plan to deploy new missiles in Europe. This resulted in huge protest demonstrations in many European capitals. In October of 1983, three hundred fifty thousand people demonstrated in London, four hundred thousand in Bonn, three hundred fifty thousand in Rome, one hundred fifty thousand in Brussels, and two hundred twenty thousand West Germans formed an unbroken human chain of protest that extended sixty-five miles from Stuttgart to Neu Ulm.

Volga Peace Cruise

The Citizen Diplomacy Volga Peace Cruise trips that were organized by Howard and Alice Frazier of Promoting Enduring Peace involved around one hundred fifty Americans and twenty or so Soviet citizens and speakers that had been selected by the Soviet Peace Committee. Promoting Enduring Peace organized and directed the trips, and cosponsors included the Association of World Citizens (AWC), Women's International League for Peace and Freedom (WILPF) and other peace groups in the U.S.

The trips began in Moscow and, after a few days, moved to Rostov on the Don where the participants boarded the passenger boat Alexander Pushkin for an eleven hundred mile trip up the Volga River, all the way from Rostov on the Don to the city of Kazan.

The 1983 peace cruise was very special because of the Moscow peace rally and the various other peace rallies held along the Volga River. After Moscow, the next joint meeting was held in the City of Rostov and featured a highly decorated war veteran who gave an emotional speech on how he could never go to war against Americans because of his memories of serving with U.S. soldiers against the Germans in World War II. After departing Rostov, the peace boat sailed up the Volga River, stopping at times to hold joint meetings with Soviet citizens. This included stops at Volgograd, Ulyanovsk, and Kazan, the capital of the Tartar Republic. At all stops we were greeted with wonderful performances of folk music and dance. On the boat there was a very good rock and roll band that performed every night with people filling the dance floor. The band also performed every time the boat arrived at and departed from a town along the river.

The cruise ended at Kazan, and after a big public peace rally in the city park, the American group traveled by airplane to Kiev. After visiting the huge and very impressive war memorial in Kiev, the group traveled to the Bari Yar Memorial where the Germans had murdered as many as two hundred thousand people and buried them in a common trench. This memorial is highlighted by a mass of towering dark statues representing the victims. It is topped by a poignant sculpture of a doomed woman kissing a child with her hands tied behind her back, symbolizing a hope for the future.

The group then flew to Leningrad, which was later renamed St. Petersburg, for a joint meeting and a visit to the memorial cemetery where five hundred thousand people are buried in mass graves, all victims of Germany's nine hundred day siege of the city. The city of Leningrad alone lost over twice as many people as our country lost in the entire war.

While Cruising on the Volga

On board the boat during the eleven days of sailing up the Volga River, we had a series of workshops on different topics led by invited speakers and open to full discussion by everyone attending. The discussions were informative as they included an exchange of views and perceptions, some of which had been badly misunderstood by both sides prior to the discussions.

On the 1984 Volga Peace Cruise, we held another joint peace demonstration in the city of Volgograd on the Volga River. This city was formerly named Stalingrad, the site of the famous battle that proved to be the turning point of World War II. The battle raged for 135 days from September 13, 1942, to January 26, 1943. The fighting was so fierce that the life expectancy on the battlefield for a Russian platoon commander was three days, and for a company commander, seven days. It was a devastating defeat for Nazi Germany, and it spelled the end of Hitler's dream of conquest. The Germans would not win another major battle in the war. The casualties in the decisive battle of Stalingrad were enormous. The Germans lost one hundred forty-seven thousand men and ninety-one thousand were taken prisoner. The Red Army had as many as five hundred thousand casualties.

The memorial to the fallen Soviet heroes is stunning. The memorial park is seen from a great distance, as this is the site of the spectacular statue "Motherland," also known as "Mother Russia," by sculptor Yevgeny Vuchetich. This statue is two times higher than the Statue of Liberty, and at the center of the memorial park is the Hall of Valor, constructed in the form of a cylinder. The walls are carved with the names of seven thousand people who died in the battle, which is only a small percentage of the total casualties. In the center of the hall, a huge hand emerges from the ground, holding a torch lit with the eternal flame. Around the top of the hall is the inscription: "We were mere mortals, and not many of us survived; but we did our duty to the Motherland." The music of Schumann's Reverie plays softly and continuously in the background.

There are many impressive statues in the memorial park, including a very poignant sculpture of a mother holding her son, a fallen soldier. Other displays depicting the horrendous battle are as impressive for the incredible courage of Soviet soldiers as they are sobering for the terrible waste of human life on both sides.

The Press Conference

The 1984 Volga Peace Cruise continued its way up the Volga River and ended at Kazan, where the American group flew back to Moscow. The following day, a press conference was scheduled at the Metropole Hotel to explain to the media the purpose of our trip, which was to build understanding and friendship and, most important of all, to accept our countries' differences as well as their similarities, including the need for peace.

All the major U.S. media stationed in Moscow came to the press conference, including ABC, NBC, CBS, the *New York Times*, and the *Los Angeles Times*. It was a room packed with cameras and reporters. Three of us led the conference and explained the purpose of the trips, but it wasn't long before the atmosphere became somewhat inquisitorial. At one point, the reporter for ABC actually asked us what side we would fight on if there were a war between our two countries. This infuriated everyone in our group, especially a contingent of World War II veterans, who came on the trip to participate in a joint memorial with Soviet veterans.

What is most interesting about this conference is that it was never reported in the U.S. media. We learned this before we arrived home, as there was a cameraman on the airplane out of Moscow from one of the TV networks. He told us that nothing would appear on TV or other media because, after we left the press conference, a *New York Times* reporter stood up and told everyone to kill the story. They dutifully followed orders, and the important story of Americans and Soviets working for peace was not reported to the American people.

This was the second time that the *New York Times* killed a story in which I was involved. In 1978, I drafted a resolution for the World Citizens Assembly in Paris that was addressed to the 1978 United Nations Special Session on Disarmament. I got forty-two Nobel Laureates to sign the resolution, and with a few colleagues, I presented it to the director of the Disarmament Center in a brief ceremony at the United Nations. The *New York Times* sent a reporter and cameraman and covered the entire story including a copy of the resolution with names of all the Nobel Laureates, but nothing appeared in the newspaper. This was all the more infuriating as the resolution was about the critical issue of nuclear weapons. Moreover, in 1978 there were not so many Nobel Laureates as today, and we may have gathered the largest number of Nobel Laureate signatures on any document up to that time. The United Nations accepted the document for its important conference, but not the *Times*. This ongoing problem with the press and its suppression of worthy news is even more extreme in this sixth year of the new millennium, as corporate America now owns nearly all the media. The press is only free if you own it, and that is not democracy.

Many interesting, and sometimes dramatic, events took place on the Volga Peace Cruises, on which I continued to participate as a speaker every year from 1983 to 1989. I should mention that the trips were handled through a travel agency selected by Promoting Enduring Peace and open to everyone interested in participating on a first-come, first-serve basis. The participants, with the exception of the trip directors and selected speakers, paid their own way, the cost about the same as regular visitor tours to the Soviet Union.

Meeting on the Volga

In 1985, another boat of the same size and carrying about the same number of passengers approached our vessel. At the time we didn't realize that the captains of the two ships had communicated by radio and decided to tie up along side one another. It turned out the other ship was carrying tourists from West Germany. When the ships were side by side, we all eagerly talked to each other and exchanged souvenirs.

Suddenly, out of the blue, one of the West German men jumped down between the ships, and from one end, started walking with one leg straddling each ship. Soon afterward, a

Soviet man did the same thing at the other end. It was a dangerous, spontaneous stunt, and the captains of the ships were understandably not happy about it. But after about five very nervous minutes, the two men safely met at the center of the boats and embraced. On both boats, we all cheered, including the captains. The drama of this story is that both men were veterans of World War II, on opposite sides of course, and this event took place with the site of the battle of Stalingrad clearly in the background.

Unforgettable!

Down the Mississippi River

In 1986, we agreed that it was time for the Soviets to visit the United States on a peace cruise just like the Volga cruises. Promoting Enduring Peace organized the cruise to travel down the Mississippi River from St. Paul to St. Louis on the legendary Delta Queen steamboat. The trip included one hundred twenty-seven Americans from twenty-seven states and forty-seven Soviet citizens from eight cities and four republics.

There were many memorable moments on this trip, although it got off to a shaky start at a press conference in Minneapolis when some right-wing goons tried to break up the meeting. But later that night, all the participants of the peace boat were invited as special guests to the premiere concert of Canto General. This is a work by the Greek composer Mikis Theodorakis based on verses of the great Chilean poet Pablo Neruda. A symphonic orchestra and chorus performed the concert. Before the program began, the Soviet participants were introduced and given a standing ovation by the two thousand people in the audience as a gesture of friendship and peace.

The morning we began the voyage, a giant Mississippi River thunderstorm threatened our departure. We didn't expect anyone to be waiting to greet the boat at the first stop. But to our surprise, hundreds of people were waiting to greet the Soviet guests and the citizen diplomacy mission. And just as we arrived, the sun suddenly broke through the clouds, and it became a beautiful day. This was an omen for the rest of the trip, which was very successful.

All along the way, thousands of people came to greet the boat to extend their own message of peace and friendship. They often waited for hours in pouring rain or searing heat with homemade signs, handshakes, and countless smiles. They did this at every town the boat passed by from Minnesota to Wisconsin, to Iowa, and on to Missouri. At each town there was an official ceremony complete with folk singers, dancers, high school bands, and speeches by elected officials.

At Davenport Mayor Thomas Hart had a Soviet and American delegation to his home for lunch. At Dubuque, Governor Terry Branstad gave the greetings and spoke at a lavish picnic in honor of the peace boat. I'll always remember the conclusion of Governor Branstad's speech, when an elderly, well-dressed gentleman came up to me and said how happy he was to be attending this event because he had never seen a Russian before, and he realized that they are just like us. A bit later he asked where I was from. He said he had never seen a Californian before, but he didn't say they are just like us. That's asking for too much, I suppose.

All the peace boat delegates were invited to tour the impressive John Deere factory in Dubuque, where the Soviets had a great time inspecting and playing with the huge tractors made in the factory. When the tour was over and we left the factory, I got on the bus carrying most of the Soviet delegates. As we got ready to depart, a young Dubuque police officer with a broad smile entered the bus and apologized to the Soviet delegates because they had showered him with souvenirs and he had nothing to give them in return. At this point, retired Soviet General Michhail Milshtein, a recent guest on the CBS *60 Minutes* television program, asked the young policeman if he could have a bullet from his gun as a souvenir. The young officer was happy to give the general one of his bullets, but now all of the Soviets on the bus wanted a bullet. Always smiling, but worried what his superiors were going to say, the policeman gave away all of the bullets in his gun and then his cartridge belt. At this point, the Russian General jumped to his feet and proclaimed this was a historic moment, the first step in unilateral disarmament between our two countries. This comment was greeted with great laughter from everyone, including the young police officer, who departed the bus amid cheers.

Goodwill and entertainment continued at each town we visited along the great river. The Soviets brought their nationally known singer, Tatyana Petrova, who at every occasion brought the crowd to its feet with cheers and pleas for more songs.

Perhaps the most impressive parts of the trip occurred at the many locks where the Delta Queen stopped along the river. Here hundreds of people, after learning through television and newspapers that the peace boat was coming, would wait to convey their own message of peace. This occurred at all hours, often late into the night, but always with a spontaneous response of folk and antiwar songs. Typical was the lock near Red Wing, Minnesota. Here, the Soviet cosmonaut Gregory Grechko leaped over the boat's railing to shake hands with the crowd. Grechko was a national hero in the Soviet Union, but the reception he received in Red Wing, Minnesota could not have been more sincere if he had landed his space capsule in the middle of Red Square.

One of the American speakers, Rear Admiral Gene LaRocque (U.S. Navy Ret.) said, "Our goal is to avert nuclear war. If we take even one step in that direction, it will be worth it." The trip was more than worth it, and with the Soviet delegation that, along with Grechko, included a famous retired general now working for peace, a famous actress and poetess, journalists, writers, and a milkmaid who was also a member of parliament. They all went back to tell their citizens that Americans want peace. A Soviet TV crew was aboard the boat to film a documentary that was shown on primetime Soviet television. An Australian TV crew and two independent American film crews were also on board to make films of the trip.

The logo of the Mississippi Peace Cruise is a drawing of the Alexander Pushkin and Delta Queen joined together with American and Soviet flags waving together, representing the notion that we are all "in the same boat." And this slogan remains true today, as we will either sink together in an eventual war, or we will have the wisdom to swim together to build a better, safer world.

Now the great difference between the Mississippi Peace Cruise and the Volga cruise was that the U.S. media covered the former extensively. They followed the boat all along the way with reports that were positive and broadcast on all the national television news, as well as many newspapers across the country and a two-page article in *Time* magazine. We were on the CBS *Morning* show and on the NBC *Today* show, where I substituted for Admiral LaRocque (who had to leave for a meeting in Washington, D.C.) and interviewed together with retired Soviet General Mikhail Milshtein.

A humorous incident occurred as the general and I were being set up with a microphone for the *Today* show. The interview was held outside the boat, and with a helicopter hovering overhead, it was very noisy. As the small microphones were attached to our shirts, we were instructed to talk to the technicians in the sound truck to make certain the sound was clear. This lasted for several minutes, and during this time, I mentioned to the general that I was happy that another host was going to interview us rather than the regular host for the program (I'll skip the name) because he often asks silly questions. At the time, I didn't know our microphones were open to the station studio in New York City and heard by everyone there, including the regular program host. The technicians in the sound truck thought this was funny. Now what's interesting is that when you are on the *Today* show, a company takes a photograph from the recording, and you can buy it for a small fee. I paid the fee and waited several weeks for the photograph to arrive by mail, but it never came. Eventually a letter arrived from the company stating that for unknown reasons the records for the day I was on the show were missing. Strange!

Back on the Mississippi

In 1988, another U.S./Soviet citizen diplomacy trip was held on the Mississippi River, again on the Delta Queen, but this time from St. Louis to New Orleans, thus completing the entire length of the Mississippi River. Aboard the boat were one hundred twelve Americans from twenty-two states, and forty-eight Soviet citizens from eleven republics in the USSR. The group included a retired general and admiral, along with professors, journalists, farmers, physicians, and people from many walks of life.

Beginning in St. Louis and moving on to Memphis, Vicksburg, Greenville, and New Orleans, where the Soviets rushed to the French Quarter to hear authentic American jazz, southern hospitality was first-rate. City governments along the route presented honorary citizenship certificates to each of the Soviets, or gave the leader of the delegation, Cosmonaut Grechko, the key to the city. Grechko, after two Mississippi River cruises, had acquired keys to several cities.

At the national military cemetery in Vicksburg, a solemn ceremony presided over by retired U.S. Navy Rear Admiral Gene Carroll and retired Soviet Major General Evgeny Nozhin made history. Here the soil from a cemetery in the USSR memorializing Soviet soldiers in World War II was scattered by a park official in a symbolic reminder of how Americans and Soviets, as close allies, defeated the

Nazi war machine and saved Western civilization as we knew it.

Meeting Gorbachev

A second peace cruise in 1988 took place on the Dnieper River in the Ukraine, ending at the capital city of Kiev. As on the Volga River trips, the boat stopped at towns along the way for citizen-to-citizen meetings. After the cruise, we returned to Moscow and were informed that we would be taken to the Kremlin for a meeting with President Gorbachev. This cruise was a special event, as it was comprised of about two hundred representatives of peace organizations from twenty-six Western countries, including thirty-five Americans.

The meeting with Gorbachev took place just a few hours after the conclusion of the Reagan/Gorbachev Moscow Summit, and it was broadcast live on Soviet television. The meeting began with Gorbachev's assessment of the summit. He emphasized that he could not agree with President Reagan on human rights and noted that great progress has been achieved by the Soviet Union, but that the West has given it neither credit nor recognition. He went on to stress that the Soviet Union has its own roots and spiritual values, which go back for centuries, and the country is proud of its past accomplishments.

When he was finished, Gorbachev looked to the audience and said, "Let's talk." For the next two hours, he listened to forty-four speakers. Everyone who desired to speak could do so, and many were long and repetitive, while others were more concise.

When my turn came I thanked Gorbachev for taking the lead in encouraging people to think and act globally so we can build a better world for the twenty-first century. I congratulated him for supporting the United Nations and for his suggestion to improve this world organization to help resolve our common global problems and for recognizing that the United Nations is an integral part of humankind's future.

After hearing so many people speak, Gorbachev ended the program by giving a spontaneous, thirty-minute summary of our meeting, causing much laughter by saying the meeting ended with more questions than when it started and that he didn't know how to close our conversation.

Among his comments:

New realities call for tolerance and a new way of looking at the world. In this context, Gorbachev mentioned the ideas expressed in his book *Perestroika* and commented that his ideas are not messianic or grandiose, but confront the new realities.

We must move to a single human civilization bound to a single organism, and this requires new ideas, which search for the better world benefiting all people.

Gorbachev commented that this meeting convinced him that diplomats do not have a monopoly on ideas and that citizen diplomacy is an element to be recognized in international politics.

Politics are lagging behind science, lagging behind technology, and lagging behind the peace movement.

Present conditions put the focus on U.S./USSR relations, but other nations must be included. Great changes are taking place in Latin American, Africa, and Asia.

The underlying policy of the USSR is reaching a nuclear weapons-free, non-violent state.

Each country and people has the wisdom to solve its own problems. We have no specific pupils or teachers, but rather we are all pupils, and history is the teacher.

The three-hour meeting ended with Gorbachev telling us that the ice had been broken and that we must now continue toward our goals. The Secretary General left the auditorium amid a thunderous standing ovation.

It's a shame that the ideals expressed by Gorbachev, including the comment that government must dialogue with the peace movement, are lost with the demise of Gorbachev as a superpower president. Moreover, with few exceptions, today's world lacks leaders with a profound vision and great intellect. More on this issue in a later chapter, but this situation makes the role of citizen diplomacy even more urgent in these decisive early years of the new millennium.

In 1989, we made another Citizens Diplomacy Peace Cruise to the USSR. This was the last of the peace cruises organized by Promoting Enduring Peace and co-sponsored by the Association of World Citizens. This year we noticed many changes taking place in the Soviet Union due to Gorbachev's *Perestroika*. But the lasting memory of the trip occurred when we stopped along the Dnieper River to visit a huge shipbuilding complex. As we toured the facilities and the new ships under construction, we noticed a huge freighter that was complete and ready to sail. The destination was Cuba, and the ship was named after the Argentine/Cuban revolutionary Che Guevara, with Che's name placed in large letters at the bow of the ship. Only one thing was wrong. My wife Noemi, an Argentine, noticed that they had misspelled Che's last name. We brought this to the attention of our guide and her superior, who remained skeptical about the misspelling. Eventually we reached a higher authority who, to his shock, realized the mistake. The name was corrected before the ship sailed to Cuba, thus averting a major embarrassment to the Soviet Union and Cuba. This was a small but important contribution of citizen diplomacy. The task today is to spread this kind of people-to-people-to-government peace building process across the globe.

CHAPTER 4
World Citizenship—The Key to the Future

I am a citizen, not of Athens or Greece, but of the world.
—Socrates (5th Century B.C.)

Prior to my Vietnam War protest years, I established a small organization called World Citizens for World Law. The only memorable achievement was the printing of a page-long letter to the editor in the *New York Times*. Years later, around 1968, I discovered that other organizations were involved in World Citizenship activities, with the most notable organization called the World Citizens Registry in Paris. This group was organized by Gary Davis, who declared himself a World Citizen at a large gathering in Paris in 1948, which received considerable media coverage, and Guy Marchand, a bright and energetic Frenchman who ran the organization for many years.

In San Francisco, I learned of other activists with a world perspective, including a real gentleman with old-world good manners. His name was James Mundstock, another activist senior citizen, and together we initiated a branch of the

World Citizen Registry, and a new activist organization we
named the World Citizens League. For several years, we held
public meetings, marched together as world citizens in anti-
war demonstrations, and distributed literature on the subject.
When Mr. Mundstock died, he was replaced by another
activist senior citizen, Alfred Williams, a retired architect who
to this day, at ninety-nine years, continues his peace activity
by attending meetings, writing letters to editors, and more.

In 1974, I received a call from two visitors from Japan to
meet them at the Hilton Hotel in San Francisco; they
represented a group of World Federalists in Tokyo. The
purpose of the meeting was to request that the group host a
World Citizens Assembly in San Francisco to commemorate
the thirtieth anniversary of the United Nations. The idea
originated at a peace conference in Japan that was attended
by Dr. Walker Bush, a colleague of ours working at the
Mankind Center in Los Angeles. At the conference Dr. Bush
and other delegates agreed that the Assembly should be held
in San Francisco and decided to request our organization host
and organize it. I thought that this was a great idea and agreed
to go do it when promised that at least one hundred people
would be attending from Japan, all paying the registration fee,
which would provide the necessary funds to begin the task of
organizing this international meeting.

World Citizens Assembly One

The first World Citizens Assembly was held at San
Francisco State University from June 20 to June 25, 1975, and
to our great surprise, over three hundred delegates from
twenty-six counties and eighty organizations registered on
opening day. This caused a great deal of anxiety, as we had
only anticipated about two hundred people from fifteen or so

countries. However, due to the great effort of the organizing committee, the first day and the rest of the Assembly moved ahead without any problems. Moreover, this first World Citizens Assembly was memorable for the great spirit and optimism that it generated.

As the chairperson for the assembly, I invited the Soviet Peace Committee to send a delegate to our conference. With little news concerning the invitation to the meeting, I did not think there would be a representative due to visa problems with the State Department. However, shortly after the meeting opened, two men in blue suits entered the auditorium and identified themselves as representatives of the Soviet Peace Committee. It turned out that one of the delegates was Valentin Berezhkov, a former translator for Joseph Stalin and later a diplomat to the Soviet Embassy in Washington, D.C.

Shortly after the conclusion of this very successful conference, we phased out the World Citizen League and named the organization World Citizen Assembly, complete with an international steering committee and secretariat in San Francisco, based on the structure of the United Nations. I had the title of Secretary General, and Dr. Lucile Green, a professor of philosophy, was named President. Some years later we changed the name to Association of World Citizens and used an organizational structure of President, Secretary, Treasurer, and Executive Board.

The secretary for more than ten years was another senior citizen named Lori Southgate, and in her late nineties, she continues to work for a better world. Our longtime treasurer to this day is Martha Killebrew, another senior with an impressive background as businesswoman and head of a Red Cross chapter. She is a woman who suffered through several personal tragedies, but always kept a cheerful and optimistic attitude. This is more evidence of the role that senior citizens have performed in the peace movement, and a story that needs to be told again and again.

Dr. Harry Lerner is another great peace worker still going strong as a senior citizen. Harry was, for many years, our UN representative, and he has been a major contributor at all AWC events.

One of the featured individuals at the San Francisco World Citizens Assembly was Shinichi Kato, a Japanese journalist and one of the first people to visit the inner city of Hiroshima after the atomic bomb dropped on August 6, 1945. Mr. Kato was a resident of Hiroshima and was saved only because of a late train to work on that fateful day. Mr. Kato said, "I was waiting for the paper in line for a tram at a suburban station, when there was a sudden green flash and I was thrown to the ground by a thunderous explosion. Dazed, I crawled away and then began to run. Scrambling over the fallen roof of the baggage room, I fled toward the mountains and so missed seeing the huge mushroom cloud over Hiroshima." When he traveled to the city, he was stunned by the horrible devastation and death; his once vibrant city had been instantly turned into a graveyard. What he experienced when he returned determined his future: "I will serve the rest of my life for peace."

Rear Admiral Arnold True, U.S. Navy (Ret.), addressed the Assembly and reminded everyone of the incredible destructive power of modern weapons, particularly emphasizing the suicidal nature of nuclear weapons. Admiral True said that it is time for people to change their way of thinking and for nations to change their obsolete political arrangements. He said that only a world system can cope with modern technology and problems and outlined the fundamental issues as: (1) elimination of nuclear weapons; (2) abandonment of war as a method of settling disputes; (3) control of the population; (4) increasing food production; (5) finding safe sources of energy; (6) conserving rather than exploiting the earth's resources; and (7) controlling pollution of the air, earth, and water.

Admiral True concluded with a deathbed quote by Socrates saying, "I am not an Athenian or Greek, but a Citizen of the World," and a quote by Huston Smith who said, "We have come to the point in history when anyone who is only a Japanese or only an American, only an Oriental or only a Westerner, is but half human; the other half of his being, which beats with the pulse of all mankind, has yet to be born."

Other invited speakers included Jean-Michel Cousteau, architect and ocean explorer; Dr. Soichi Iijima, President of Hiroshima University; Dr. Carlton Goodlett, Physician and Publisher; Jerry Voorhis, former U.S. Congressman; and Dr. Kazuteru Hitaka, the leader of the Japanese delegation and Director of the United World Federalists of Japan, who stated, "Brothers and sisters, my dear world citizens from east and west, from all parts of the world, let us act now; let us move now; let us join together hand in hand to create one interdependent world community."

Messages

The following telegraph was read in the opening session:

To Douglas Mattern, Chairman Planning Committee World Citizens Assembly.

*Looking for Square Two: Moving from War and Organized
Violence to Global Community*

On behalf of the president I send greetings to all those
attending the World Citizens Assembly being held on the
thirtieth anniversary of the founding of the United
Nations.

We are convinced that the peoples of the world
recognize the approaches are needed to resolve the urgent
questions of world peace, security, and development with
which your meeting is concerned.

Your agenda is challenging, and it is our view that such
intellectual dialogue and people-to-people contact serve to
promote international understanding and to contribute
toward a more peaceful world.

Best wishes for a successful meeting

Sincerely,
John E. Reinhardt
Assistant Secretary for Public Affairs
Department of State
Washington, D.C.

From the Mayor of San Francisco:

Greetings from San Francisco Mayor Joseph L. Alioto.
The year 1975 marks the Thirtieth Anniversary of the
founding of the United Nations. The City of San Francisco
is proud to be the birthplace from the curse of war and to
harness all available resources of energy and knowledge for
the needs of all.

The welfare and security of all of the citizens of San
Francisco is linked with the security and welfare of all
communities in the world, and that the threat of war to
any community is a threat to all humankind; and our
objectives in San Francisco must be to continue
individually and collectively in encouraging our citizens to

recognize their citizenship responsibilities and to extend it to the entire world community.

On behalf of all San Franciscans it gives me great pleasure to extend greetings to all attending the World Citizens Assembly, 1975. We in San Francisco are certain the conference will be productive for all concerned.

Joseph L. Alioto
Mayor of the City and County of San Francisco

We had a great evening of entertainment led by George Cory, the composer of "I Left My Heart in San Francisco," which is San Francisco's official anthem. Other entertainment featured Korean singer Sook II, American tenor Carl Hague, a Court Dance from Thailand, and a Japanese folk ensemble that prepared a dance performance especially for the Assembly.

Leaders of various faiths, including Sikh, Hindu, Buddhist, Shinto, Jain, Vedic, and Christian, gave their messages of peace. Symbolic trees were planted at the university as a tribute to the World Citizens Assembly with the following plaque in front of the trees:

Through interdependence to world community these trees are presented in commemoration of the World Citizens Assembly, July 1975, and thirtieth anniversary of the founding of the United Nations in San Francisco.

World Citizens Assembly Two

The next World Citizens Assembly was held in Paris from July 1 through July 5 in 1977 and was attended by over five hundred people from twenty-five countries, including representatives from socialist and third world countries, as well as United Nations observers and a representative from President Jimmy Carter's office based in the American Embassy in Paris.

The first session was held at Sorbonne University with opening remarks by Nobel Laureate Alfred Kastler. Delegates gave short greetings along with supportive telegrams. Pierre Elliot Trudeau, Prime Minister of Canada, made this statement:

> I am pleased to extend my warmest greetings as you gather in Paris for the World Citizens Assembly. We on the North American continent enjoy a high standard of living. However, the welfare and dignity of others will be the measurement of our own condition. We must be ready to accept the challenges of poverty, hunger, environmental degradation, and nuclear proliferation. These issues will determine the stability of tomorrow's world. They will require innovative solutions and co-operative endeavor in our common cause of global dimensions. I would remind you of Thomas Paine's words of two centuries ago: "My country is the world, and my religion is to do good." I know that you will be discussing these issues and wish you fruitful deliberations.

After the meetings at the Sorbonne University, the entire Assembly moved to complete the conference at Cite Universitaire with the opening session at Maison Internationale. The keynote speaker was Robert Maller, Rector of the Universities of Paris, and Chairman of the World Association for Scientific Responsibility, who called for a new spirit of leadership among the world's people. Delegates spent the next three days discussing environmental issues, stopping the arms race, meeting basic human needs, and supporting a strong United Nations.

The entire Assembly, along with a selected panel, was invited to hold a special session in the French Senate, and on the final day, we were given a champagne reception by the French Government in the same palace that was to receive the United Nations Secretary General the following day.

World Citizens Assembly Three

The third World Citizens Assembly was held in Japan from July 27 through August 6, 1980, with the theme of "Acting Together to Build a World Community." Along with a large delegation from Japan, more than one hundred fifty delegates attended, including fifty from Europe, fifty from the U.S., fifteen from India, and smaller numbers from Mexico, the Sudan, Thailand, Australia, Canada, and the Soviet Union.

The opening session in Tokyo was held in beautiful Horinkaku Hall, and delegates began working on how people and organizations can work with governments to resolve the growing serious problems confronting humanity. During the meetings, the Governor of Tokyo invited the entire Assembly to a lavish reception that included long tables with a large variety of food and drink.

The Assembly then moved on to a second meeting in the City of Osaka. Here the host was Rev. Toshio Miyake, who played a major role in the 1975 Assembly in San Francisco. As we arrived at Konko-Kyo Church of Izuo, Rev. Miyake's church, we were met by a line of hundreds of children with flags and colorful dress, along with bands playing and people greeting us with smiles and salutations.

The second Japan Assembly session was held in the church with more than one thousand in attendance. Messages of greeting were read from the Mayor of Osaka and Nobel Peace Laureate Phillip Noel-Baker, who was in Japan to speak in Hiroshima on August 6.

The culmination of this one-day session was the adoption of the Osaka Declaration appealing for all peace organizations to work together for the common cause. At the session's end, we were given a great reception with a large variety of food and drink and a candlelight farewell as the entire Assembly moved on to Hiroshima.

Deep in the Mountains

Prior to arriving in Hiroshima, Lucile Green and I were taken by car on a lengthy ride deep into the beautiful mountains, eventually arriving at a Buddhist Monastery. On arrival we were taken to a room and were instructed on the rituals of an elaborate and spiritual tea ceremony we were to take with a Buddhist monk.

After the tea ceremony, we went to the church, and I noted the absence of any people other than a few Buddhist monks. We seemed to be, as they say, in the middle of nowhere. But then deep sounding drums and bells broke the stillness, and soon hundreds of people seemed to materialize, filling the large auditorium in the temple. Dr. Green and I gave presentations on our assembly and the quest for a more just and peaceful world for the coming years. After our speeches the Buddhist priests performed a very moving and beautiful religious ceremony that I will never forget.

Hiroshima

The Japan Assembly concluded with a two-day session and adoption of some pertinent documents, including my Hiroshima Resolution with its fifty-one Nobel Laureate endorsements. This resolution was presented to the UN Disarmament Center and accepted as a document for the 1982 UN Special Session on Disarmament.

On August 6, the entire Assembly attended the thirty-fifth commemoration of the atomic bombing of Hiroshima. I put this experience into the following article I wrote for the Japan Assembly:

Children of Hiroshima

The third World Citizens Assembly was scheduled to conclude in Hiroshima so that all delegates could participate in the annual August 6 Memorial Day Commemoration. This year in Hiroshima the mood was particularly somber due to the ominous escalation of the nuclear arms race and the war clouds that seem to loom on the horizon.

As we gathered with forty-thousand people in Peace Park, where thirty-five years ago a nuclear fireball instantly incinerated this city and forever changed human history, the historical tragedy that lingered was tangible. And as the bells of Hiroshima tolled for the victims in deep and haunting tones, we realized that in some way they toll for all of us, that we are children of Hiroshima.

After the official ceremony, long lines formed to visit the Memorial Museum located in the park. This is a museum like no other. It contains many photographs taken soon after the bomb exploded.

There are also accurate models of the city before and after the bomb, as well as other artifacts of that fateful day in history. The devastation is awesome.

All are searing reminders that nuclear weapons have a destructive capacity beyond our comprehension. This takes an even sharper focus when we remember that the atomic bomb of Hiroshima was quite small compared to the hydrogen bombs of today, and that the present stockpile of nuclear weapons now equals well over one million Hiroshimas.

The Memorial Museum is proof that anyone who accepts the use of nuclear weapons for any reason is history's biggest fool. My own thought after leaving the museum was that every general, every admiral, every politician who holds or aspires to high national office should be required to visit the museum once a year and make his reaction public.

As evening descended on the city, thousands of people made their way to the river adjoining the park. They came to place colorful paper lanterns in the river. Many write the names of the victims on the paper, symbolizing that their souls will be freed when the lanterns make their way to the open sea.

By darkness, thousands of lanterns made a silent procession floating down the river. It was a colorful yet sorrowful scene, and we sensed that the lanterns represented all of us—humanity striving to reach a rational sea, freed from the nuclear terror that haunts our time.

The ceremony in the park, the ringing bells, and the lanterns were all viewed against a background of a modern and thriving city. It was a scene that clearly reflects the major contradiction of the twentieth century: great progress, which has changed our way of life more in a few decades than in all previous history, contrasted with a terrible destruction manifest in scores of brutal wars and the slaughter of 100 million people.

Hiroshima symbolizes this latter aberration. And yet the bomb that laid this city to waste, and the far more powerful bombs in our current arsenals, are not the deadliest weapons.

As a recent UNESCO publication so pointedly stressed, the deadliest weapon is the human brain that has created all the vast means of destruction witnessed in the twentieth century.

This, of course, is the same brain that is responsible for our creative acts, for art, for science, for love of each other and life itself, for civilization, and for the determination to find just solutions to our many global problems. This latter point was also evident in Hiroshima on August 6. During the afternoon more than ten thousand people filled a gymnasium to capacity for another peace rally, while another two thousand people waited outside, unable to get in.

The highlight was Lord Philip Noel-Baker's ascension to the podium. At ninety years of age, his body was frail and he required much help to reach the microphone. His mind and spirit, however, were magnificent.

In a surprisingly booming voice, Lord Baker denounced those escalating the arms race and preparing for war. He implored everyone to oppose these policies and engaged all ten thousand people to chant, "No more war." The chant reached a rafter-shaking crescendo that could have been heard around the world.

This was Hiroshima on August 6, 1980, and it demonstrated a startling truth: that humankind is engaged in its most telling contest between the two aspects of the human brain. The heritage of violent struggle that emanates from our long evolutionary past is pitted against our creative intelligence that is lifting us to higher consciousness. Cognizant of this crisis, Hiroshima Mayor Takeshi Araki issued a plea to the nuclear powers urging them to come together in a Peace Summit: to resolve the growing threat posed by the arms race.

Looking for Square Two: Moving from War and Organized Violence to Global Community

When we returned home we found little response from our government to Mayor Araki's proposal. On the contrary, there were new and dangerous policies announced, such as Presidential Directive 59, along with a plethora of cold war rhetoric.

It is without question that disarmament with security is the most crucial issue of our time. It is a complex problem that covers the entire spectrum from converting the armament industry to peaceful products, to building a strong and representative United Nations made capable to settle disputes between nations and peoples through the framework of world law. There is no alternative to perpetual war and eventual ruin for humankind.

To achieve this goal, all of us, as the children of Hiroshima, must work together with sufficient pressure to force a change in the course of world events. It requires that we reject all propaganda and political opportunism that attempts to divide us from our common needs.

We can no longer be enemies to each other, for the children of Hiroshima have but one option: to build a world community with justice, lasting peace, and a future.

Postscript: The Soviet Peace Committee sent two delegates to the Japan Assembly. One was an official of the peace committee and the other was a journalist who came primarily to visit Hiroshima as he was adamantly against nuclear weapons. On the evening of August 6, my wife, Noemi, and I strolled through the park with the two Soviet delegates exchanging views on a variety of subjects.

The one issue on which we agreed was that nuclear disarmament is the most important issue of our time. We ended the night sharing a few vodkas with some caviar. A few years later the Soviet journalist became a regular feature on

U.S. television news and interview programs. His name is Gennadi Gerasimov, the press secretary for President Mikhail Gorbachev. We like to think his visit to Hiroshima as a delegate to the World Citizens Assembly had some influence on his steady opposition to nuclear arms as Gorbachev's press secretary. We will meet Mr. Gerasimov again at a later World Citizen Assembly.

The next Assembly was held in 1984 in Los Angeles at the time of the Olympic Games. Later, several World Citizens Assemblies were held in New York City, during which time the organization expanded with branches in thirty-five countries, and the organization's name was changed to Association of World Citizens. We also created a new World Citizen ID card that is carried by people in more than forty countries. The card looks like a passport, but it is in fact a symbol of being a responsible Citizen of the World.

More Assemblies

Four World Citizen Assemblies were held in New York in close proximity to the United Nations, as the Association of World Citizens (AWC) has non-government organization (NGO) status with the United Nations Department of Public Information (DPI) and Consultative Status with the United Nations Economic and Social Council (ECOSOC). We have NGO delegates in New York, Geneva, Bangkok, Addis Abba, and the Hague.

The New York sessions were devoted to supporting UN programs and expanding the organization. During these meetings, we had several high-ranking officers of the United Nations as keynote speakers:

Dr. Robert Muller, Assistant Secretary General who was, and remains, a great supporter of our activities; Erskine

Childers, Senior Advisor to the UN and Director General for Development and International Cooperation; Abdelkader Abbadi, Director of Political Affairs for the UN Department of Political and Security Council Affairs; Dr. Alexander Borg Oliver, the father of the Climate Control Convention at Rio and Principal Officer in the UN Department of Humanitarian Affairs; as well as other UN officers, all of whom gave inspiring and very informative presentations.

Back to San Francisco

World Citizen Assembly number ten was held once again in San Francisco at San Francisco State University from June 17 through June 21, 1995, in commemoration of the fiftieth anniversary of the birth of the United Nations.

This conference got off to a sad start because, of the ninety-nine individuals from Africa that registered for the Assembly, only two received visas from the U.S. State Department. Some other meetings taking place in San Francisco as part of the UN celebration also had this problem with the State Department. The usual response from our government was a concern that some of the people from developing countries might not return home after the meetings. This was ridiculous, considering that every day hundreds of people illegally crossed the border from Mexico. Moreover, most of the delegates from Africa and Asia who were denied visas had proven reputations for working for peace and human rights and attending many conferences in Europe and other countries.

It was, nevertheless, a successful and memorable Assembly. Keynote speakers included Jorge Wertheim, Director of UNESCO at the United Nations, and a special guest that we so fondly remembered from the 1980 World

Citizen Assembly in Japan, Gennadi Gerasimov, the former press secretary for President Gorbachev.

A special evening was set aside to present the Reverend Jesse Jackson with a special World Citizen Award for his prominent work in human rights in both the United States and other countries. Rev. Jackson accepted the award and gave an inspiring speech before seven hundred people at the University.

Entertainment was provided by noted jazz musician Eddie Gale, the AWC Ambassador of Music. Mr. Gale put together a jazz orchestra to play his original work. Also performing was Laura Williams, the singing voice of Nala in the movie *The Lion King*. The American Indian, Jake Swamp, internationally known for his tree planting ceremony, led the planting of a tree at the university in honor of the fiftieth anniversary of the United Nations and twentieth anniversary of the World Citizen Assembly.

One sunny afternoon all the participants were taken by bus to walk across the Golden Gate Bridge. For years, we received letters from individuals telling how much they enjoyed the wonderful walk on the bridge with the grand view of San Francisco and the bay's surrounding hills.

Celebrating World Citizenship
In 1999, I decided that rather than organize another World Citizen Assembly, it was time for World Citizenship to be recognized as an annual event. And after about six months of organizing, we held the event on the first day of spring of the new millennium, March 20, 2000, and it was San Francisco that took center stage as host of the first World Citizenship Day. Nature contributed to this premier event with a beautiful sunny sky and just enough wind to flutter the more

than one hundred world citizen flags at the celebration. The event was held in Joseph L. Alioto Performing Arts Piazza.

A special World Citizen Award was presented to San Francisco Mayor Willie Brown Jr. The award honored Mayor Brown for his work fighting for racial harmony and civil rights and for having the vision and global perspective to designate World Citizenship Day in San Francisco. With the help of the mayor's staff we created the following World Citizenship Day Proclamation.

PROCLAMATION—City and County of San Francisco

WHEREAS, peace is of the utmost importance to everyone, and begins when we respect each other, mother earth and ourselves; and

WHEREAS, senseless loss of life can be eliminated once we establish a vision of world peace in concurrence with nonviolent solutions to world differences; and

WHEREAS, in order to create a "culture of peace" in the Global Village of the 21st century, we need to think and act as responsible citizens of the world; and

WHEREAS, world citizenship is the unifying principle capable of transcending racial, ethnic, and political differences that divide humanity; and

WHEREAS, the City of San Francisco, the birthplace of the United Nations, joins the global community in celebrating World Citizenship Day; now

THEREFORE BE IT RESOLVED that I, Willie L. Brown Jr., Mayor of the City and County of San Francisco do hereby proclaim March 20, 2000 as

WORLD CITIZENSHIP DAY IN SAN FRANCISCO

IN WITNESS WHEREOF, I have hereunto set my hand and caused the Seal of the City and County of San Francisco to be affixed.

San Francisco is famous for its colorful events, and World Citizenship Day more than met this standard. Nearly four hundred performers of the Tai Ji Men, under the direction of Dr. Hong Tao Tze, traveled directly from Taiwan to participate in World Citizenship Day. They came with huge drums, artistic dragons, and beautiful costumes to perform spectacular dances and songs for over two hours with San Francisco's City Hall looming in the background. Coinciding with the event, a new AWC branch was established in Taiwan with Dr. Hong as director and Honorary Vice President of AWC.

Jazz musician Eddie Gale performed with a sixteen-piece jazz orchestra playing his original composition entitled "Children of Peace." Youth were represented by a large contingent of students from local schools.

Dr. Hong brought the organization's beautiful and very large bronze peace bell, which could be heard throughout the Piazza reverberating the theme of peace and friendship. Mayor Brown and I were asked to ring the bell and add our names on its surface. As of 2005, this peace bell has traveled to many regions of the world and has been rung by national presidents, vice presidents, governors, mayors, parliamentarians, Nobel Peace laureates, United Nations officials, and noted peace activists. Their signatures are all engraved on the surface of the bell.

World Citizens Assembly 2001

World Citizens Assembly Eleven was held in Taipei, Taiwan from March 30 to April 2, 2001, in the spectacular Grand Hotel. This was one of the largest Assemblies to date, with four hundred delegates attending from fifty-two countries. We held a World Citizenship Day celebration during the Assembly that was held in Taipei Stadium and attended by twenty thousand people with some four hundred performers. The president of Taiwan, Chen Shui-bian, was the keynote speakers and declared all 23 million Taiwanese as world citizens on this date. The Vice President of Taiwan, Annette Lu, also spoke at this event and attended several sessions of the World Citizens Assembly.

The host committee, the AWC branch in Taiwan under the leadership of Dr. Hong Tao Tze, organized a wonderful and very memorable event, complete with lavish entertainment and a great party for all the delegates.

The theme of this Assembly was "Creating a Culture of Peace for the Twenty-first Century." Workshops were held on the crucial issues, and the Assembly produced "Peace Declaration 2001," signed by over five hundred thousand people.

Keynote speakers at the 2001 WCA included Dr. Charles Mercieca, President of International Association of Educators for World Peace; Dr. Hong Tao Tze; myself; and Dr. Rashmi Mayur, Director of International Institute for Sustainable Future and a vice president of the Association of World Citizens. Just about one year after this conference, Dr. Mayur, who traveled to ninety-two countries working for a sustainable environment and peace with justice, died from the effects of a stroke he suffered at the 2002 UN Summit Meeting in Johannesburg, South Africa. As one of the key players in the peace and world citizens movement, Dr. Mayur's passing was a tragic loss to our common cause.

Back to Taiwan

Due to the success of the Taipei World Citizens Assembly, Vice President Annette Lu of Taiwan wrote me a letter requesting the Association of World Citizens to sponsor a peace conference to be held in Taiwan from August 14–15, 2001. I readily agreed and once again traveled back to Taiwan.

Five Nobel Peace Laureates were featured at this conference: Joseph Rotblat, Oscar Arias Sanchez, Lech Walesa, Jody Williams, and F.W. de Klerk. After two days of intense discussion, a terrific entertainment program was held in a large, modern, outdoor theater with several thousand Taiwanese in attendance.

Human Manifesto

In 2003, at the suggestion of AWC Project Director Lola Kristof, who personally experienced the utter brutality of war and has become totally devoted to creating a better world, we revised the Human Manifesto document that was originally issued in 1972 with the endorsement of many distinguished individuals. With the permission of the now defunct organization Planetary Citizens and its chairman, Donald Keys, we decided to reissue this great document with a new set of endorsers. The text is brief but very pertinent for our world in 2006. Endorsers of this new issue include Presidents Jimmy Carter and Gerald Ford, Boutros Boutros-Ghali, Walter Cronkite, the Dalai Lama, Jane Goodall, conductors Mstislav Rostropovich and Zubin Mehta, Dr. Robert Muller, Astronaut Edgar Mitchell, Bishop Desmond Tutu, Oscar

Arias Sanchez, Mario Cumo, and many other notable personalities.

A HUMAN MANIFESTO

Human life on our planet is in jeopardy.

It is in jeopardy from war that could pulverize the human habitat.

It is in jeopardy from preparations for war that destroy or diminish the prospects of decent existence.

It is in jeopardy because of the denial of human rights.

It is in jeopardy because the air is being fouled and the waters and soil are being poisoned.

It is in jeopardy because of the uncontrolled increase in population.

If these dangers are to be removed and if human development is to be assured, we the peoples of this planet must accept obligations to each other and to the generations of human beings to come.

We have the obligation to free our world of war by creating an enduring basis for world peace.

We have the obligation to safeguard the delicate balances of the natural environment and to develop the world's resources for the common good.

We have the obligation to place the human interest, and human sovereignty above national sovereignty.

We have the obligation to make human rights the primary concern of society.

We have the obligation to create a world order in which man neither has to kill or be killed.

In order to carry out these obligations, we the peoples of this world assert our primary allegiance to each other in the family of man.

We declare our individual citizenship to the world community and our support for a United Nations capable of governing our planet in the common human interest.

The world belongs to the people who inhabit it. We have the right to change it, shape it, nurture it.

Life in the universe is unimaginably rare. It must be protected, respected, cherished.

We pledge our energies and resources of spirit to the preservation of the human habitat and to the infinite possibilities of human betterment in our time.

The struggle continues for people to think and to act as responsible Citizens of the World. The future depends on it.

CHAPTER 5
There's No Business Like War Business

In the sixth year of the new century, many of us stand bewildered by what happened to the wonderful expressions of hope and joy that were expressed in the millennium celebrations. Today the world is a mirror image of the twentieth century, which was among the most brutal and destructive in human history. A major factor is that the war business promotes militarism and conflict while producing enormous financial profit. A tragic indicator of the values of our civilization is that "there's no business like war business."

World military spending in 2003 was $956 billion. By 2005 it became a trillion dollar a year business in what is surely history's most irresponsible and criminal allocation of wealth and resources. Every day nearly $3 billion is spent on the means to destroy one other, while at the same time half of humanity lives on about $2 day, and 1 billion people in extreme poverty exist on less than $1 a day.

Thirty-two high-income countries account for 75 percent of world military spending, and the United States leads all others nations by a wide margin. The Center for Arms

Looking for Square Two: Moving from War and Organized Violence to Global Community

Control in Washington, D.C. reports the following comparison between military spending by the United States and the rest of the world. Figures compiled from 2004 to 2006. The U.S. budget is for Fiscal 2006, and does not include funds for nuclear weapons that are annually included in the Department of Energy Budget or supplemental funds for the wars in Iraq and Afghanistan.

Country	Military Budget (in $ Billions)
United States	419.3+
Russia	65.2
China	56.0
United Kingdom	49.0
Japan	45.1
France	40.0
Germany	29.7
Saudi Arabia	19.3
India	19.1
Italy	17.5
South Korea	16.4
Australia	11.7
Turkey	11.7
Israel	10.8
Canada	10.1
Spain	9.9
Brazil	9.2
Netherlands	7.7
Taiwan	7.5
Greece	7.2
Indonesia	7.6
Sweden	5.9
North Korea	5.5
Ukraine	5.5

Singapore	5.0
Poland	4.4
Norway	4.4
Kuwait	4.2
Iran	3.5
Belgium	3.3
Pakistan	3.3
Colombia	3.2
Portugal	3.2
Vietnam	3.2

Twenty-one additional countries are listed, all under $3 billion as annual military spending. Add up the total for all countries, and it turns out the United States spends nearly as much on the military as all the other countries combined.

Just think of all the missiles, bombs, et cetera that will be replaced for profit by the armament industry after the current U.S. military assault on Iraq. In the first fourteen days, the U.S. dropped over 8,700 bombs, including more than 3,000 cruise missiles.

Cruise missiles cost over $500,000 each. The Apache Longbow Helicopter costs about $22 million each. The Bradley Fighting Vehicle costs over $1.2 million. Each B-1 Stealth bomber costs over $2 billion.

Tim Weiner reported on the front page of the August 19, 2005, edition of the *New York Times* that the new CVN-21 aircraft carrier costs an estimated $13.7 billion. A smaller George H.W. Bush Nimitz-class aircraft carrier costs $6.1 billion. The new Virginia-class submarine is estimated to cost $2.5 billion each, and a new guided missile destroyer, Arleigh Burke-class, cost over $1 billion each.

Looking for Square Two: Moving from War and Organized Violence to Global Community

The latest obscenity in the war business is the decision by the Bush Administration to sell F-16 Fighter Jets to Pakistan. The administration has offered to sell the same jet fighters to India, always a potential adversary. But selling weapons to both sides of a conflict is standard policy. In 1999, the U.S. supplied weapons or military training to parties in thirty-nine of forty-two active conflicts.

Profits are up, morality is down; there's no business like war business!

Data compiled by the Federation of American Scientists shows that since 1992, the U.S. exported over $142 billion dollars worth of weapons to states around the world. The data also reveals that the world market is dominated by the U.S., accounting for nearly half of all weapon sales in 2001. That is more than $12 billion dollars for U.S. manufacturers. The Center for International Policy estimates that about 80 percent of U.S. arms exports to the developing world go to non-democratic regimes.

Other leading nations in this "merchants of death" business include Russia, France, Great Britain, China, Germany, and to a lesser degree, Sweden, Israel, Belgium, Belarus, Italy, and North Korea, to name a few.

For U.S. companies, the real profits come from the annual defense budget. For the fiscal year of 2006 the Bush Administration is requesting $78 billion for procurement of military goods; the majority of this going to the research and development of new weapons. Steven Kosiak, director of budget studies at the Center for Strategic and Budgetary Assessment, says, "We've come to the point where we're spending more money than we spent during the Cold War."

William D. Hartung and Michelle Ciarrocca provide an excellent description of how the weapons industry works with the government regarding the weapons business. Hartung says, "These have been boon years for the arms industry, with contracts for the top weapons contractors up 75 percent in the first three years of the Bush administration alone." As the director of the arms project, Hartung reports: "While some of this funding is related to the war in Iraq or the campaign against terrorism, much of it relates to the Cold War relics like the F-22 combat aircraft or nuclear attack submarines that have little or no application to the threats we now face or the wars we are now fighting."

Regarding election contributions by the weapons industry, the report found that, of the more than $13 million donated to the 2004 election, 62 percent went to Republican candidates and 38 percent went to Democratic candidates or committees. The report also details the presence of former executives and consultants of weapons contractors in key policymaking positions in the Bush administration. This includes at least thirty-two administration appointees that were involved in the arms industry, seventeen of which were linked to major defense contractors. The military establishment and the armament industry seem to have developed a revolving door.

The Top Pentagon Contractors in Billions of Dollars*

Company Rank	2004 Contracts	2001 Contracts
1. Lockheed Martin Corporation	20.7	14.7
2. Boeing Company	17.1	13.3
3. Northrop Grumman Corp.	1.9	5.2
4. General Dynamics Corporation	9.6	4.9
5. Raytheon Company	8.5	5.6

6. Halliburton Company	8.0	0.4
7. United Technologies Corp.	5.1	3.8
8. Science Applications Int. Corp.	2.5	1.7
9. Computer Science Corporation	2.4	0.4
10.Humana Inc	2.4	0.4

*Data collected by the World Policy Institute and U.S. Department of Defense

The top lobbyist for the 2000 elections was Lockheed Martin at $2.8 million. This is the world's largest military contractor and perhaps the world's most powerful corporation. In 2001, Lockheed had $14 billion in sales of weapons to the U.S. and foreign buyers. Moreover, Lockheed received a $3.5 billion contract to sell F-16 jet fighters to Poland. As a new member of NATO, Poland, along with Hungary and the Czech Republic, agreed to modernize their military and purchase new weapons. For the Lockheed sale, the U.S. Government loaned Poland $3.8 billion, obviously to purchase the Lockheed planes. The expansion of NATO is a vehicle to sell U.S. weapons, and not surprising, the weapons industry is the biggest lobbyist for NATO expansion.

In the councils of government, we must guard against the acquisition of unwarranted influence, whether sought or unsought, by the military-industrial complex. The potential for the disastrous rise of misplaced power exists and will persist.
—President Dwight Eisenhower

The *New York Times* reports that in 2001 Lockheed had $32 billion in sales and was number one in Pentagon contracts with $21 billion. Number two was Boeing with $17 billion, followed by Northrup Grumman with $11 billion.

The *Times* article quotes Robert H. Trice Jr., a senior vice president, who commented that Lockheed's global reach is growing. The article reports that with its dominant position in fighter jets, missiles, rockets, and other weapons, Lockheed's technology will drive the security spending for many American allies in coming decades. The article continues by stating that Lockheed sells aircraft and weapons to more than forty countries, and that the American taxpayer is financing many of those sales. As an example, Israel spends much of the $1.8 billion in annual military aid from the United States to buy F-16 warplanes from Lockheed.

The article reports that in the future Lockheed hopes to build and sell hundreds of billions of dollars (yes, billions) worth of the next generation of warplanes, the F-35. Known as the Joint Strike Fighter, Lockheed got the contract valued at $200 billion, the largest project ever funded by the Pentagon.

Another Lockheed vice president, Tom Burbage, said the day will come when everybody will be flying the F-35s with anticipated sales of four thousand to five thousand planes.

There's no business like war business.

CorpWatch (www.corpwatch.org) reports that Lockheed Martin did not receive the huge F-35 contract by design alone. In 2000, the company spent over $9.8 million lobbying members of Congress and the Clinton administration. One of Lockheed's new lobbyists was Haley Barbour, the former chairman of the Republican National Committee.

Lockheed has a criminal record, as if making weapons for profit were not enough. In the 1970s the company admitted to paying $22 million in bribes to win overseas contracts.

Some ten years ago Lockheed admitted paying $1.2 million in bribes to an Egyptian official to seal the sales of Lockheed cargo planes.

The sale of weapons that is turning our planet into one giant arsenal is extremely profitable. The arms merchants were formerly called "merchants of death." But today, they consider themselves savvy businessman selling any type of weapons they can to just about any government that will buy them.

The Council for a Liveable World reports that in 2000, worldwide arms sales totaled $36.9 billion, with the U.S. accounting for $18 billion in sales, or more than 50 percent. Russia was second with $7.7 billion, and France was third with $4.1 billion. The *New York Times* reports in an article on August 30, 2004, that by 2003 worldwide sales had dropped, although they were still enormous, and again the U.S. led this sad parade with $14.5 billion or 56 percent. As usual, Russia was next in the profit line with $4.3 billion.

The five exporters of major conventional weapons from 1999 to 2003 were, in order, the U.S., Russia, France, Germany, and the United Kingdom. There was no shortage of clients. The Stockholm International Peace Research Institute (SIPRI) reports that there were nineteen major conflicts in eighteen locations in 2003. In the fourteen-year post-Cold War period, there were fifty-nine different arms conflicts in forty-eight different locations. We can be sure that the arms merchants from all the major countries were involved in providing the weapons for every conflict.

There's no business like war business, including the small arms trade that totals between $4 and 6 billion per year. The leading exporters in terms of value are the U.S. and Russia. But this business is spread around the world, with over one thousand companies in some ninety-eight countries involved in the production of small arms and ammunition. Small arms kill over five hundred thousand people a year in conflicts.

The lucrative business of weapons extends down to rifles and handguns. There are more than 65 million handguns in the U.S., and some 192 million in total firearms. In 1998 alone, dealers sold an estimated 4.4 million guns in the U.S., nearly 2 million of them handguns. The result was 12,102 firearm murders.

This world in arms is not spending money alone. It is spending the sweat of its laborers, the genius of its scientists, the hopes of its children. This is not a way of life at all, in any true sense. Under the cloud of threatening war, it is humanity hanging from a cross of iron.
—President Dwight Eisenhower

Taking the War Business to Space—The End of Freedom

The United Nations took the lead in proclaiming that space should be reserved for peaceful purposes through the Outer Space Treaty of 1969. This treaty includes the following principles as summarized by the UN Office for Outer Space Affairs:

The exploration and use of outer space shall be carried out for the benefit and in the interests of all countries and shall be the province of mankind;

Outer space shall be free for exploration and use by all States;

Outer space is not subject to national appropriation by claim of sovereignty, by means of use or occupation, or by any other means;

States shall not place nuclear weapons or other weapons of mass destruction in orbit or on celestial bodies or station them in outer space in any other manner;

The Moon and other celestial bodies shall be used exclusively for peaceful purposes;

Astronauts shall be regarded as envoys of mankind;

States shall be responsible for national space activities whether carried out by government or non-governmental activities;

States shall be liable for damage caused by their space objects; and

States shall avoid harmful contamination of space and celestial bodies.

In 2000, a General Assembly document called the "Prevention of Outer Space Arms Race" was adopted by a vote of 163 to none. Great so far, but the bad news is there were three abstentions to this resolution: the United States, Israel, and Micronesia.

The U.S. abstention was expected as this country has definite plans to move into space with the National Missile Defense project being just the first step. Lawrence Kaplan says we should drop all the pretenses and admit that missile defense is about preserving America's ability to wield power. It's not about defense, it's about offense and that is why we need it.

The agency in charge of weapons in space is the U.S. Space Command, created during the Reagan Administration. The Commander-in-Chief of the U.S. Space Command, General Joseph Ashy, made the purpose of the Space Command perfectly clear:

It's politically sensitive, but it's going to happen. Some people don't want to hear this, and it sure isn't in vogue, but—absolutely—we're going to fight in space. We're going to fight from space, and we're going to fight into space. That's why the U.S. has development programs in directed energy and hit-to-kill mechanisms. We will engage terrestrial targets someday—ships, airplanes, land targets—from space. (*Aviation Week and Space Technology*, August 9, 1996)

And Keith Hall, Assistant Secretary of the Air Force for Space, stated in a speech to the National Space Club in 1977: "With regard to space dominance, we have it, we like it, and we're going to keep it. Space is in the nation's economic interest."

The following is from the U.S. Space Command (USSPACECOM):

Vision 2020: Control of Space Global Engagement Full Force Integral Global Partnership

Control of Space is the ability to assure access to space, freedom of operations within the space medium, and an ability to deny others the use of space, if required. Space is recognized as the fourth medium of warfare. Joint operations require the Control of Space to achieve overall campaign objectives. The Control of Space will encompass protecting US military, civil, and commercial investments in space. As commercial space systems provide global information and nations tap into this source for military purposes, protecting (as well as negating) these non-military space systems will become more difficult. Due to the importance of commerce and its effects on national security, the United States may evolve into the guardian of space commerce—similar to the historical example of navies protecting sea commerce. Control of Space is a complex mission that casts USCINCSPACE in a classic warfighter role and mandates an established AOR.

The Ability to Dominate Space

The Almanac published by the Space Command declares that "tomorrow's air force will likely dominate the air and space around the world." The economists wrote that "the long promised transformation of the American defense system from a cold war fighting force to the high tech arms race of the future is finally going to take place."

The arms industry is diligently working to develop new space weapons with contracts that will extend for decades. One of the weapons under development are Space Rods, sometimes called "Rods from God," that are platforms in space orbit with tungsten rods around twenty feet in length and a foot in diameter. Jack Kelly, *Post-Gazette* National Security Writer, reported the rods could be guided by satellite to targets on Earth, striking at speeds of around twelve thousand feet per second that would destroy hardened bunkers several stories beneath the surface. No explosives would be needed. The speed and weight of the rods would lend them all the force they need.

Other weapons under development include space-based lasers, microwave guns, and a weapon that would illuminate the battlefield with light that only one side could see. The Rand think tank report entitled "Space Weapons, Earth Wars" describes more exotic, future space-based weapons.

Directed-energy weapons consisting of laser, radio frequency, and particle beam weapons. The soft targets would be located from the surface of the earth to space.

Kinetic-energy weapons against missile targets are designed to destroy hardened targets above sixty kilometers and moving at high speed by "lethal impact."

Kinetic-energy weapons against surface targets designed to destroy hardened and slow-moving targets on the earth's surface.

Space-based conventional weapons against surface targets consist of space-based conventional weapons aimed at fixed or moving targets on the surface or in air.

Just what kind of a world will it be if our last frontier, space, is blocked by weapons of war orbiting the planet twenty-four hours a day? Is this the end of freedom and the beginning of non-stop fear as we gaze to the stars and the mystery of the universe above, only to see orbiting platforms loaded with weapons?

Soviet Cosmonaut Aleksandr Aleksandrov wrote the following while in orbit:

> One morning I woke up and decided to look out the window to see where we were. We were flying over America and suddenly I saw snow, the first snow we ever saw from orbit. Light and powdery, it blended with the contours of the land with the veins of the rivers. I thought autumn, snow-people are busy getting ready for winter. A few minutes later we were flying over the Atlantic, then Europe, and then Russia. I have never visited America, but I imagined that the arrival of autumn and winter is the same there as in other places, and the process of getting

ready for them is the same. And then it struck me that we are all children of our Earth. It does not matter what country you look at. We are all Earth's children, and we should treat her as our mother.

We cannot allow a chain of weapons to circle our mother Earth; thus the militarization of space must be stopped before it is forever too late.

CHAPTER 6
Still the Best Hope—The United Nations

To that world assembly of sovereign states, the United Nations, our last best hope in an age where the instruments of war have far outpaced the instruments of peace, we renew our pledge of support—to prevent it from becoming merely a forum for invective—to strengthen its shield of the new and the weak—and to enlarge the area in which its writ may run.
—President John Kennedy

I still find amazing and troubling the negative attitude of so many American citizens and elected officials regarding the United Nations. I find that this is mostly due to an appalling lack of knowledge about this world institution, and partly from a limited perspective of the world in which we live. People often condemn the UN for the actions it takes as if the UN were a separate organization divorced from national governments. This is not the case. The UN is comprised of national governments, and they make the decisions for the UN to carry out. When people are displeased with UN voting, they should vent their anger at the governments that cast the vote and not the staff of the UN. The UN is an organization of states to be used for the purposes for which it was created.

News and information about the myriad of activities of this world organization are regularly reported in the media of most countries. It's quite the opposite in the United States, where very little positive news concerning the United Nations is reported in the mainstream press. In many states, the United Nations is omitted from the school history books. A few years ago I presented lectures on the United Nations to several high schools and discovered that not only did the students lack knowledge about the UN, but their teachers did too. The only good news was that the majority of the students were interested and eager to learn more about this vital organization.

In the developing world, which comprises the vast majority of humanity, the blue flag of the UN is welcomed and recognized as people helping people to resolve crucial issues. "In the developing countries, the UN doesn't mean frustration, confrontation, or condemnation," said Ecuador's delegate to the organization, Miguel A. Albornoz, "it means environmental sanitation, agricultural production, telecommunications, the fight against illiteracy, the great struggle against poverty, ignorance, and disease."

Many of the people who work for the UN in its humanitarian efforts often have to endure very difficult and sometimes dangerous conditions. These heroic people should be honored and recognized for their work. Focusing on individuals that make a real contribution to humankind might help to overcome the superficial, celebrity-worshipping culture that is so dominant in our country today.

The United Nations is a vast organization that operates in every corner of our world through its principle organs and many agencies and programs. Perhaps the most important accomplishment of the United Nations is that it has universal membership, which is the first step in the difficult task of establishing a world community for the twenty-first century.

As in any organization, there is need for change and reform. The UN's chief architect, President Franklin Roosevelt, said as much in his last speech before Congress: "No plan is perfect. Whatever is adopted at San Francisco will doubtless have to be amended time and again over the years, just as our own Constitution has been. No one can say exactly how long any plan will last. Peace can endure only so long as humanity really insists upon it, and is willing to work for it, and sacrifice for it."

And today, reform is the chief concern with the United Nations. Secretary General Kofi Annan commissioned a high-level panel of experts to recommend structural changes so that the UN could be more efficient in meeting difficult challenges in the coming years. After receiving their report, Mr. Annan called on world leaders to approve the most sweeping changes to the United Nations since it was founded sixty years ago.

The panel came up with many proposals for reform, including a recommendation to expand the Security Council to be more representative of the world's people. The panel recommended two options for change. One would add six new permanent members, and the other would create a new tier of eight semi-permanent members: two each from Asia, Africa, Europe, and the Americas. From the beginning there have been five permanent members to the Security Council: United States, Russia, China, France, and England, each country having the power to veto. The remaining states rotate to comprise the fifteen-member Security Council.

Kofi Annan also proposed a comprehensive anti-terrorism strategy, urging world leaders to unite behind a definition of terrorism and adopt a comprehensive convention against it. Regarding development, Mr. Annan urged the rich countries to honor the commitment that was reached by consensus at the Millennium Summit 2000 to allocate 0.7 percent of gross national product for development assistance by 2015. The United States has one of the lowest levels: about 0.15 percent. All member states of the United Nations agreed to a set of Millennium Development Goals to be reached by the year 2015.

The summit meeting considering these recommendations was held at the United Nations in New York City from September 14 to 16, 2005, and attended by presidents, prime ministers, and kings from 151 member states. Only a week before the meeting, it appeared the conference might be a complete failure that would be a devastating blow to this world organization. Several countries were causing problems in opposing the suggested reforms, including expansion of the Security Council. At one point it seemed that John Bolton, the new U.S. Ambassador to the UN, had virtually ruined any chance of success when he proposed a myriad of changes to the recommended proposals. Bolton did manage to eliminate the commitment of all nations to work for the elimination of nuclear weapons, which was clearly the biggest defeat for the conference. Secretary General Kofi Annan called this failure a "real disgrace."

President Bush made a conciliatory speech at the summit and stated the U.S. supported the United Nations. This was a significant change in attitude from the Bush's previous speeches at the UN. The U.S. also agreed to support the Millennium Development Goals to the great relief of the conference, although it is unclear if the U.S. is committed to providing the specific amount of funds outlined in the original Millennium Declaration. Nevertheless, an outright rejection of these goals by the U.S. would have dealt a terrible blow to the world's poor and to the UN itself.

The thirty-five-page declaration that was approved by the consensus of all nations focuses on the following items:

A new human rights council to replace the present Commission on Human Rights that had been widely discredited. The specifics of the council will be formulated in the General Assembly.

Establishment of a peace-building commission that will deal with post conflict country development.

On terrorism the document condemns it "in all its forms and manifestations."

On management reform the document accepts the goal of more outside oversight auditing of the UN and its institutions.

Regarding development, the existing "Millennium Development Goals" are affirmed with the promise to reduce poverty by one-half for the poorest of the poor by the year 2015. However, the specific commitment by developed countries to provide 0.7 percent of their gross national product to fund development was omitted under pressure of the United States.

Although Secretary General Kofi Annan and other officials were disappointed that many of the proposed reforms were not accepted, others believe that the Summit was successful as a first step toward further reform and an affirmation that the UN has a critical role to perform in the world community for the foreseeable future.

The most important lesson from this conference is that non-government organizations (NGOs) must make a much bolder effort to convince their governments to give full support for the UN and for needed reform. Too many organizations that are established to support the UN tend to support their government policies instead, even when such policies are clearly detrimental to the UN and its mission. In addition, the UN needs to be more representative, including some type of a Peoples Parliament to serve as an advisory body to the General Assembly and to provide a moral voice regarding decisions and programs. The parliament could be comprised of existing organizations that already have NGO status with the UN's Economic and Social Council. Former UN Secretary General Perez de Cuellar recommended a two-chamber General Assembly, one chamber for government representatives, as at present, and the other representing national civil society organizations.

One thing is clear: The United Nations has a vital role to perform in the crucial years ahead. It is the only international institution that, with full support, can realistically lead to the global governance that is imperative to meet the great challenges ahead. These include the establishment of enforceable international law to end the war business, disarmament, eradication of poverty, and the foundation for the new civilization that is mandatory for the twenty-first century.

The UN Every Day

The United Nations has produced more international law than any organization in history, and few people are aware of its profound effect on their lives every day. This includes such mundane matters as mailing international letters. It's the UN agency named the Universal Postal Union (UPU) that sees that your mail is delivered.

Another UN Agency, the International Civil Aviation Organization (ICAO), has greatly helped to make flight the safest mode of travel. The International Maritime Organization (IMO) has made great contributions on safety for ships at sea. And thanks to this UN agency, pollution from tankers has been reduced as much as 60 percent.

Other UN agencies such as UNICEF, UNESCO, the World Health Organization (WHO), the UN Development Program (UNDP), the High Commissioner for Refugees (UNHRC), the UN Peacekeeping forces, and so many others perform a vital role each and every day for the entire world community. The list and definition of these agencies can be found in Appendix A.

The American people can be proud that it was President Franklin Roosevelt who first envisioned and determined the name of this world organization. In August of 1941, Roosevelt and Prime Minister Winston Churchill established principles based on international cooperation to achieve peace and security. This document became known as the Atlantic Charter, which represented a kind of blueprint for the UN. The full history of the UN can be found in Appendix A. This section also includes the organization's structure, how the UN works, a list of important accomplishments, and the full text of the UN's Universal Declaration of Human Rights.

CHAPTER 7
Albert Einstein: Scientist, Peace Activist, World Citizen

When we consider the vast problems now confronting humanity and the sweeping decline in vision and ideals, Einstein's knowledge, dedication, and encompassing insights take on a new meaning for our time. Albert Einstein was more than a great scientist; he was one of the greatest intellects in history. Moreover, he was equally a great human being, a true citizen of the world who devoted a large part of his life to working for peace and justice.

Einstein's peace work is important to recall at this critical time in history, and for this reason I have included a chapter on this great man. The year 2005 was the one hundredth anniversary of his greatest scientific breakthrough, which forever changed our understanding of the universe. His scientific contributions are enormous, but his Theory of Relativity is one of the great epoch-making concepts in all of human history. As a scientist, he had a unique ability to see deeper and more comprehensively than most of his peers. Perhaps this was rooted in his profound respect for nature: "My religion consists of a humble admiration of the illimitable superior spirit who reveals himself in the slight details we are able to perceive with our frail and feeble minds."

Einstein's Special Theory of Relativity was published in 1905. It caused an immediate stir in the scientific community, although few realized the full revolution it would have on our understanding of the physical world. Einstein developed the theory through a long chain of mathematical reasoning and an incredible ability to visualize in his mind the physics of our world. In his time, scientists didn't even know what galaxies were, and yet today, scientists use Einstein's theories to understand a universe of more than 100 billion galaxies and other objects in the universe that were totally unknown before.

The Special Theory of Relativity basically asserts that there is no "absolute space" or "absolute time," that the universe has no fixed points of reference. All motion and physical behavior must be considered relative to some arbitrarily chosen frame of reference, and no frame of reference has priority over any other.

The second assertion of the special theory is that light always travels with the same constant velocity regardless of the motion of the observer or the source of the light. Light travels at a speed of one hundred eighty-six thousand miles per second.

The single most important result of the special theory, in Einstein's opinion, was the understanding that mass and energy are equivalent and interchangeable. This was expressed through Einstein's famous formula $E=MC^2$, where the energy (E) of a given particle is equal to the mass (M) of that participle multiplied by the speed of light, and then again by the speed of light (C^2). This formula underlies much of nuclear and elementary particle physics.

According to the Special Theory of Relativity, space and time form one inseparable unit: a space-time continuum consisting of three dimensions of space (length, width, height) and one of time.

In 1916, Einstein's General Theory of Relativity was published, which is essentially a theory of gravity. Unlike Newton's view of space and time as separate, Einstein viewed the universe as a space-time continuum in which space is warped or curved due to the presence of matter. What we call gravity is actually the condition that exists because material objects follow the easiest and most efficient course over the undulations of the curved space-time continuum.

The General Theory of Relativity provided cosmologists with new models that Newtonian physics could not handle. The four-dimensional curved space universe of Einstein has the profound property of being finite, yet without boundaries. A theoretical astronaut, for example, could travel near the speed of light for billions of years, visiting countless galaxies, yet never reach a boundary. Likewise, straight lines eventually return to themselves. This concept led the great physicist Max Born to remark: "This suggestion of a finite but unbounded space is one of the greatest ideas about the nature of the world which has ever been conceived."

The relativity theory implied that the universe is expanding, yet most scientists in the early 1900s could not accept this concept. This even included Einstein, who worked for years to find a mathematical way out of the implication of his own theory, only later to admit this attempt was his biggest scientific mistake.

It wasn't until the late 1920s that the great astronomer, Edwin Hubble, working at the Mt. Wilson Observatory, provided physical evidence that the galaxies are moving away from each other at tremendous speeds, and thus proving that the universe is, indeed, expanding. This evidence prompted cosmologist William McGrae to remark: "Einstein's theory of general relativity came into its own as a physical theory. Now it has successfully made the greatest prediction in the history of science."

Einstein's relativity theory also implied that the universe had a beginning, or a starting point. Later cosmologists developed the "Big Bang" theory, which asserts that the universe (all space, time, matter, and energy) was concentrated into a super-dense form, called a singularity, around 20 billion years ago. After a cataclysmic eruption, the singularity began expanding, eventually into the universe we know today. It continues to expand.

In 1921, Einstein won the Nobel Prize for physics, but not, as widely believed, for his theory of relativity. He received the prize for his classic analysis of the photoelectric effect, also published in 1905, which has a great influence on quantum theory and technological application in spectroscopy, television, lasers, and other byproducts of the photoelectric cell.

Altogether, Einstein published more than three hundred scientific papers and books. Even if we were to disregard the theory of relativity, Einstein's other scientific achievements would rate him as one of history's greatest scientists.

It's truly amazing that Einstein created the theory of relativity, with its remarkable understanding of the physical world, within his mind. He did not have a laboratory, astronomical equipment, or staff. The theory was conceived during Einstein's employment as a clerk in the Swiss patent office.

In this age when people in the media are foolishly labeling entertainers, football coaches, et cetera, as geniuses, they should reflect on the life of Einstein and understand what constitutes a real genius.

Einstein was born in the city of Ulm in Germany on March 14, 1879. Einstein was actually a slow learner, with difficulty speaking as late as nine years old. When he was seventeen, he decided to attend the Polytechnic Institute in Zurich, but failed the entrance exam. After he graduated in 1900, he applied for an assistant professorship of physics, but was turned down. He then landed a job in the Swiss patent office. This just goes to show one should never be discouraged. If one of the greatest geniuses in history can fail an exam, there is hope for all of us.

Einstein the Man

Einstein the man was equal to Einstein the scientist. He had a tremendous sense of humility and, like his contemporary humanitarian Albert Schweitzer, a great respect for life. Much of Einstein's time was devoted to the pursuit of peace and better relations between peoples and governments, a consequence of his firm belief that "taking an active part in the solution of the problems of peace is a moral duty which no conscientious man can shirk."

The glorification of war and militant nationalism disturbed him greatly: "Our schoolbooks glorify war and hide its horrors. They inculcate nationalism and war in the veins of our children. I would teach peace rather than war. I would inculcate love rather than hate," and further, "The fact that men have become accustomed to war preparation has so corrupted their mentality that objective and humane thinking become a virtual impossibility; such thinking will even be regarded as suspect and will be suppressed as unpatriotic." It's worth noting that the FBI compiled a thousand-page dossier on Einstein for his peace-related activities.

Einstein was a socialist, believing that the predatory phase (capitalism) of human development should be ended. He wrote a long essay entitled "Why Socialism?" which was published in the *Monthly Review* in 1949. Einstein was also a pacifist who held that one should "never do anything against conscience, even if the state demands it...." Along with Gandhi, he advocated passive resistance, but only to a point. When faced with a force that seeks to destroy society, such as fascism, Einstein firmly believed that violence is not only justified, but the only moral action possible—people of conscience cannot be passive while others are slaughtered.

War profiteers always drew his condemnation: "This political-power hunger is often supported by the activities of another group whose aspirations are on purely mercenary economic lines. I have especially in mind that small but determined group active in every nation, composed of individuals who, indifferent to social considerations and restraints, regard warfare, the manufacture and sale of arms, simply as an occasion to advance their personal interests and enlarge their personal authority." When World War I broke out in 1914, Einstein was a professor at the University of Berlin. He was disgusted by the war and the eagerness of so many of his fellow scientists to work on military projects.

One of the leading opponents of the nuclear arms race, he knew the inevitable result if nuclear weapons were not eliminated and forever outlawed. In his famous telegram addressed to hundreds of prominent Americans, printed in the *New York Times* on May 25, 1946, Einstein wrote: "Our world faces a crisis as yet unperceived by those possessing power to make great decisions for good or evil. The unleashed power of the atom has changed everything save our modes of thinking, and thus we drift toward unparalleled catastrophe...a new type of thinking is essential if mankind is to survive and move toward higher levels."

Einstein believed that the establishment of world law is imperative to achieve disarmament: "Our defense is not in armament, or in science, not in going underground. Our defense is in law and order," and further, "The establishment of a supra-national government constitutes the deepest hope for mankind. I am convinced that only when men everywhere will meet...pledged to a common law will mankind be able to conquer its despair...with all my heart I believe that the world's present system of sovereign nations can lead only to barbarism, war, and inhumanity, and only through world law can we assure progress toward civilization."

Einstein was a strong supporter of the United Nations, considering it the evolutionary path to the world law he advocated: "Under such a system the function of individual states would be to concentrate more or less upon internal affairs, and in their relations with one another they would deal only with issues and problems which are in no way conducive to endangering international security."

More of Einstein's Thoughts

It is characteristic of the military mentality that nonhuman factors (atom bombs, strategic bases, weapons of all sorts, the possession of raw materials, etc.) are held essential, while the human being, his desires, and his thoughts—in short, the psychological factors—are considered as unimportant and secondary; the individual is degraded to human material.

> Heroism on command, senseless violence, and all the loathsome nonsense that goes by the name of patriotism—how passionately I hate them!
>
> Nationalism, in my opinion, is nothing more than an idealist rationalization for militarism and aggression.
>
> A hundred times a day I remind myself that my inner and outer lives are based on the labors of other people, living and dead, and that I must exert myself in order to give in the same measure as I have received and am still receiving.
>
> The most incomprehensible thing about the world is that it is incomprehensible.
>
> The release of atom power has changed everything except our way of thinking…the solution to this problem lies in the heart of mankind. If only I had known, I should have become a watchmaker.
>
> I am absolutely convinced that no wealth in the world can help humanity forward, even in the hands of the most devoted worker in this cause. The example of great and pure personages is the only thing that can lead us to find ideas and noble deeds. Money only appeals to selfishness and always irresistibly tempts its owner to abuse it. Can anyone imagine Moses, Jesus or Gandhi with the moneybags of a Carnegie?
>
> My religion consists of a humble admiration of the illimitable superior spirit who revels himself in the slight details we are able to perceive with our frail and feeble mind. (*The American Scholar*, Summer 1947)

With all the commemoration of Einstein's scientific work in 2005, it would do humanity well to reflect on his call to individual conscience and the building of a world community where new priorities and purpose do away with war and weapons of mass destruction. This could help us meet the present crisis and move on to learn more of the infinite mysteries of the space-time universe, as well as our integral role within it.

George Bernard Shaw on Einstein

Shaw was a great admirer of Einstein. The following is a tribute he made at a dinner honoring Einstein in London in 1930.

In London great men are six-penny and are a very mixed lot. When we drink to their health and make speeches about them, we have to be guilty of scandalous suppression and disgraceful hypocrisies. Suppose I had to rise to propose a toast to Napoleon. The one thing which I should not possibly be able to say would be perhaps the most important—that it would have been better for the human race if he had never been born. Tonight, at least, we have no need to be guilty of suppression. There are great men who are great among small men. There are great men who are great among great men, and this is the sort of man that we are honoring tonight. Napoleon and other great men of his type were makers of Empire. But there is another of man who gets beyond that. They are makers of universes and as makers of universes their hands are unstained by the blood of any human being.

CHAPTER 8
Choosing Wisdom Over Fools and Folly

If liberty and equality, as is thought by some, are chiefly to be found in democracy, they will be best attained when all persons alike share in the government to the utmost.
—Aristotle

In the United States of America we must ask how we have moved so rapidly from the brilliant leadership of Franklin Roosevelt and the inspiration of John Kennedy to the dreadful leadership we have in the early years of this new millennium. This country has sadly declined from the noble democratic ideals so eloquently expressed by President Roosevelt on the role of government: "The pace of our progress is not whether we add more to the abundance of those who have much, it is whether we provide enough to those who have too little."

This ideal has degenerated to a "greed is good" philosophy and the Ronald Reagan drivel that "government is the problem." Regarding the latter, note that every time a natural disaster strikes, the same people who accepted the Reagan line, but lost property and personal goods in the disaster, are the first to demand immediate government aid. During my years working in corporations, I often heard this nonsense from managers and would-be managers who blindly accepted the corporate line that government should get out of the way and let business alone, meaning doing away with government imposed regulations.

Corporations used this tactic to convince working people that unions are bad for business, bad for them personally, and that they get in the way of the company's ability to look out for its employees' welfare. This gullible attitude persists even during periods of mass layoffs, which are often imposed only to increase the profit margins for the corporation, its executives, and its stockholders.

This anti-union tactic has been successful with the Silicon Valley corporations that are touted as industrial leaders, which is true on the technological level, but not for the majority of their employees. Most workers in the high-tech firms have no protection or anything resembling collective bargaining. In addition, many are now experiencing the consequences of one company after another eliminating their retirement plans (the ones that actually had a plan to begin with). The result is that people, many having worked twenty years or more in the Valley, find they have no retirement from their labor other that what they could save through government sponsored 401K retirement plans. And what could be saved, especially for people with large families, was often small due to the high cost of living in the area, including outrageous housing costs that only benefit the real estate companies, banking institutions, and investors.

At company meetings, it was common for employees to ask of the management if and when a retirement plan would be established, only for the company CEO to tell them that there would never be a retirement plan. At one meeting the CEO actually said he thought it best if employees worked for the company for around five years and then moved on. Of course, the CEO did not wish this for himself, although a couple of years later he was fired for poor performance, but still left with a fortune in compensation. Three times I worked for a leading Silicon Valley company where the CEO was fired for taking the company down the drain and promoting substantial layoffs, only to leave with millions of dollars in compensation. You just cannot lose when you name your own salary and stock bonus.

Corporations are also outsourcing work in developing countries solely to acquire cheap labor and unregulated working and environmental conditions. A report by the Institute for Policy Studies and United for a Fair Economy, entitled "Executive Excess 2004" shows that "outsourcing of service jobs to low-wage countries has further widened the pay gap between workers and their bosses. Currently, the pay gap between U.S. CEOs and American call center workers is 400 to 1, while the gap between U.S. CEOs and Indian call center workers is 3,348 to 1."

The study revealed that Bank of America cut nearly five thousand U.S. jobs while outsourcing up to eleven hundred jobs to India in 2003. Then in 2004, "The firm announced that it planned to cut another twelve thousand five hundred U.S. jobs in the next two years. Meanwhile, CEO Kenneth Lewis received $37.9 million in compensation in 2003, nearly 110 percent more than in 2002."

Taking data from *Business Week* magazine and the Bureau of Labor Statistics, the report found that the average CEO compensation at the fifty firms outsourcing the most service jobs increased by 46 percent in 2003. From 2001 to 2003, the

top fifty outsourcing CEOs earned $2.2 billion while sending
an estimated two hundred thousand jobs overseas. What is
most disappointing is the acquiescence of workers in this
country. The mild response to this injustice makes a deep
contrast with the moral outrage that marked the great union
movement in the early decades of the twentieth century.

> You know, the only trouble with capitalism is capitalists. They're too
> damn greedy.
> —Herbert Hoover

The corporate world took the lead in our new culture of
greed as is evident in the disgraceful scandals of Enron and
so many other companies. And it is the company CEOs who
lead the greed machine by establishing a corporate insiders
club in which CEOs appoint other CEOs and top executives
to their Board of Directors, which then rubber stamp
whatever size compensation is put on the table. This practice
moves from one company to the next.

According to *Business Week*, the average CEO salary of a
major corporation was 42 times the average worker's salary in
1980. By 1990 it increased to 85 times, by 1999 it rose to 419
times, and in 2000 CEO salary reached 531 times the average
worker's salary. Moreover, a 1999 study conducted by United
for a Fair Economy found that CEO compensation bears
little resemblance to performance. In many cases CEOs were
awarded huge payments even though the company lost
money and thousands of workers were fired. When you can
name your own salary, performance is of no consequence.

To be sure, corporations have a very important role in
society to provide jobs and products, but they have no right
to buy our politicians and then have them write the laws that

favor their business, as they do through huge campaign donations. Corporations have but one purpose and that is profit and acquisition. And with all the corporate scandals, people know there is an alarming, make that disgusting, degree of corruption in the corporate world that must be rectified.

Back to Enron, Frank Rich reported in the *New York Times* that this company used almost nine hundred offshore "subsidiaries" to avoid paying any income taxes in four of the last five years. And let's not forget Congress. Rich reports that seventy-one senators and one hundred eighty-eight congressional representatives have been on the "Enron gravy train."

In my years as a senior engineer in the corporate world, I personally knew a top position manager who was forced to resign his high-paying executive job in quality control because he could not take the constant decisions of upper management overriding quality control rejections, and then sending the product out the door for sale. His problem, of course, was that he was an honorable person, and he was not alone in this industry.

I remember well a large company meeting with all employees present to hear the plant director openly lie to his superiors and the employees that a very crucial product being developed, which was behind schedule, had just passed all tests. Cheers and salutations followed the announcement. The only problem was that the product had failed all tests. I learned this from the engineer in charge of testing the product.

Corporations often lie to cover up defective products and other discrepancies (including criminal behavior), and this is why it is so crucial that solid government regulations are put into place to stop this practice and why the multinational corporations must be bound by international law to behave in the best interest of all people. To be fair, there are a great many honest and ethical people in high positions in the corporate world who ascribe to this ideal and openly deplore any unethical practice, but only regulation bound by law can ensure it.

Regarding corporate power in our political process, I was flabbergasted to learn a few years ago that in the state of California, the laws had been changed so that any business or corporation can fire any employee without providing a reason. This is such an outrageous and unjust legislation that it could only have been passed by politicians that were bought by the corporations to serve their wishes.

What is most disturbing is that things are not getting better as corporate power and influence continues to grow. The Bush administration, for example, intends to partially privatize one of the most successful programs in the history of government: social security. Fortunately this deceitful scheme that would mainly benefit Wall Street corporations and investors is being met with tremendous resistance from all age groups and will hopefully be abandoned.

For a full perspective on what is taking place, we need to understand that social security is just one aspect of the overall goals of conservatives in this country to overturn the great social programs of Roosevelt's "New Deal" legislation and the "Great Society" legislation of later democratic administrations. The present course by the Bush administration, where policy is designed for the rich and corporate America, is rapidly eroding our democracy and setting up a plutocracy where the rich rule. David Cay Johnston is a Pulitzer Prize winning reporter and author of the book *Perfectly Legal: The Covert Campaign to Rig Our Tax System to Benefit the Super Rich—and Cheat Everyone Else.* Johnston reports that in 1993, the top four hundred highest income Americans paid thirty cents of each dollar in federal income taxes. By the end of the Clinton Administration in 2000, they were down to twenty-two cents. Under President Bush, their burden is less than eighteen cents. Everyone else's taxes rose.

Johnston explains that IRS data, adjusted for inflation, shows that the poor are really getting poorer and the rich are getting fabulously richer, a trend enhanced by their falling tax burden. Johnston reports that by 2000, the richest 1 percent had as much income as the bottom 96 million Americans. He also demonstrates that Bush's tax legislation means Congress takes money from people making $30,000 to $500,000 per year and gives it to the richest 1 percent.

Bob Herbert, columnist for the *New York Times*, writes that President Bush has proposed more than $200 billion worth of cuts in domestic discretionary programs over the next five years and cuts of $26 billion in entitlement programs. Herbert shows that funding will be cut for education; food assistance for pregnant women, infants, and children; HIV and AIDS treatment; and environmental protection programs. He concludes that "the advances in areas like education, antipoverty programs, health services, environmental protection and food safety were achieved after struggles that, in some cases, took many decades. To slide backward now (hurting millions of people in the process) because of a desire to siphon funds from those programs and hand them over as tax cuts to the wealthiest members of our society is obscene."

The divide between rich and poor has advanced to such an extent that in 2004 the congressional budget office found that the income gap in the United States is the widest in seventy-five years. And yet the rich just keep getting richer and the poor get poorer while the middle class struggles. The number of billionaires in this country, for example, increased from 179 in 1996 to 228 in 2003.

Don't Forget the Stock Market

People are constantly told that they are part of the great wealth in this country because so many Americans are involved in the stock market. This is another myth as shown in a position paper on inequality prepared by the Congressional Progressive Caucus with Representative Peter DeFazio as Chairman: "The benefits of the stock market go to few people with almost 90 percent of the value of all stocks and mutual funds owned by households is held by the richest 10 percent. An estimated 86 percent of the benefits of the increase in the stock market between 1989 and 1997 went to the top 10 percent of households, with 42 percent going to the richest 1 percent. Since the mid 1970s the top 1 percent of households has doubled their share of the national wealth from 19 percent to 42 percent."

Consider this discrepancy of wealth when we learn that teachers in this country often have to use money from their own meager salaries to help buy school supplies for their students because the school district is out of funds. The list goes on with nurses and many other professionals that are so essential in our society, but that are so poorly paid they cannot even live in the areas where they work and are faced with constant layoffs or threats of layoffs.

Healthcare is another indicator of the growing inequality. The Census Bureau reports the number of people who lack health insurance coverage rose to 45 million. This is the largest number of uninsured people ever reported since the Census Bureau began issuing data on the number of uninsured in 1987.

The exorbitant cost of medicine is another indicator. The pharmaceutical companies are free to charge whatever they want because we have a congress that does not adequately regulate this industry, in large part because so many politicians are indebted to the pharmaceuticals due to campaign donations. The result is that many people, particularity the elderly, are unable to afford the medicine they need and are often forced to choose between buying food or medicine because they cannot afford both.

It's shocking to learn that the United States has the widest discrepancy between rich and poor among Western industrial countries. Professor Edward Wolf, an economist at Columbia University, states that "we're becoming an oligarchic society, with an extreme concentration of wealth. This concentration of wealth is protected through a political process that's making it difficult for anyone but the monied class to have a voice."

This dramatic change is a betrayal of the American democracy that much of the world used to admire and often envy. It is an even greater betrayal to the American workers who fought, and sometimes died, so that their children and grandchildren could have a better life.

Most disturbing is how the Bush administration makes the conditions even worse. Former President Clinton recently warned that the federal deficit may be coming untenable. He says this is driven by foreign wars, the post-hurricane recovery program, and (remember this) tax cuts that benefited just the richest 1 percent of the U.S. population. Clinton bravely included himself in this group.

And it gets more shocking! Clinton stated that "what Americans need to understand is that every single day of the year, our government goes into the market and borrows money from other countries to finance Iraq, Afghanistan, Katrina, and our tax cuts." Clinton continued: "We have never done this before. Never in the history of our republic have we ever financed a conflict, military conflict, by borrowing money from somewhere else." He added, "We depend on Japan, China, the United Kingdom, Saudi Arabia, and Korea primarily to basically loan us money every day of the year to cover my tax cut and those conflicts and Katrina. I don't think it makes any sense."

What makes even less sense is President Bush's statement that he will not raise taxes to pay for new expenses, and more senselessly, that he will continue to cut taxes. This is a great favor to the president's rich friends and campaign donors, but a disaster for the country as a whole.

Katrina

Countless statistics and articles have failed to arouse much interest or sympathy from the majority of Americans to the plight of the poor in this country. It's ironic that Hurricane Katrina and its ensuing destruction and loss of life may have changed this. The television images of tens of thousands of people, mostly poor and black, stranded for long, hot days and dark, frightening nights without water or food, and for many, seemingly forgotten, are impossible to forget. I believe most people would agree that, had this hurricane struck an affluent and mostly white city, at least some federal aid would have arrived before the winds subsided. Perhaps some good will come from this tragedy if it exposes the wide economic class division and helps to improve race relations, as well as correcting what was total incompetence by the federal and state governments in emergency response to a major disaster.

A Wealth Tax to End the Plutocracy

Professor Edward Wolf, the author of *Top Heavy: The Increasing Inequality of Wealth in America and What Can be Done About It*, believes a wealth tax is mandatory: "I have proposed a separate tax on wealth, which actually exists in a dozen European countries. This has helped to lessen inequality in European countries." Professor Wolf proposes a progressive tax, exempting the first $250,000 of wealth. That would exclude 80 percent of all families. The wealth tax would increase at increments, starting out at 0.2 percent from about $250,000 to $500,000. The marginal rate would go up to 0.4 percent from $500,000 to $1 million and then to 0.6 percent from $1 million to $5 million and then to 0.8 percent thereafter.

Consider that, as of 1982, the wealthiest four hundred individuals in the Forbes annual ratings owned $92 billion. By 2000, their wealth increased to over $1.2 trillion, and it becomes clear that some level of wealth tax is necessary to both regain our democracy and to fund the many problems this country faces in the coming years. It's time for Congress to consider such legislation!

To counter the current trend, we need to accept that democracy cannot function when corporations have too much power. Corporations are totalitarian to the extreme, with one man or woman ruling from the top down. There is no democracy in the corporate workplace. A world run by corporations would be a disaster.

Democracy cannot function when running for high political office requires a huge resource of money for any chance of success. Statistics from the Federal Election Commission show that the average cost of winning a seat in Congress in 1996 was $3,765,000 for the Senate and $675,000 to the House of Representatives.. The total cost of the presidential and congressional elections in 2004 was over $2 billion.

It's money that wins most elections, as revealed by the Center for Responsive Politics. Their investigation found that in the 2000 congressional elections the big money spenders won the vast majority of the races. Consider the shocking statement by Sen. Ernest F. Hollings (D-S.C.) that fundraising for all senators "distracts us from the people's business…It corrupts and degrades the entire political process…Fundraisers used to be arranged so they didn't conflict with the Senate schedule; nowadays, the Senate schedule is regularly shifted to accommodate fundraisers."

It's also evident that democracy cannot function when the media, which should operate for the benefit of the people, is owned and run by a handful of corporations. This guarantees the suppression of ideas, cleverly accomplished by the corporate-run media by simply ignoring people with progressive ideas, keeping them off the airwaves, and thus restricting their exposure to the public.

The Media

People don't know what is happening, and they don't even know they don't know.
—Noam Chomsky

The reason that people have so little knowledge is that the mainstream media is now owned by a handful of corporations that control television and radio stations, publishing companies, newspapers, movie studios, and more, and the vast majority are mainly focused on presenting corporate interests and acquiring maximum corporate profit. For this reason, most programming is designed to appeal to the lowest common denominator in terms of culture. This is why so many movies and television programs are written to appeal to the teenage audience, because that particular faction has control over their parents, and thus the parents' buying power.

A major criticism of the U.S. media came from BBC Director-General Greg Dyke: "Personally I was shocked while in the United State by how unquestioning the broadcast news media was during the war [in Iraq]." Mr. Dyke singled out Fox News as the worst offender among the stations for its "gung-ho patriotism."

One of the country's most respected journalists, Bill Moyer, had this to say about freedom of the press:

"If you think there is freedom of the press in the United States, I tell you there is no freedom of the press....They come out with the cheap shot. The press should be ashamed of itself. They should come to both sides of the issue and hear both sides and let the American people make up their minds."

Just Who Owns the Media?

The following is a list of the major media conglomerates and a small sample of their holdings, but keep in mind that the holdings periodically change as the media giants acquire new companies.

TIME WARNER

Television: CNN, HBO, Turner Classic Movies, TBS Superstation

Books: Time Life, Book of the Month Club, and 23 other book brands

Movies: Warner Brothers Studios

Magazines: *Time*, *Life*, *People*, *Sports Illustrated* and over 20 other magazines

Music: Warner Music Group with over 40 labels

WALT DISNEY COMPANY

Television: ABC and ABC Radio, ESPN

Books: Walt Disney Publishing

Movies: Walt Disney pictures, Touchstone Pictures, Miramax Films, Buena Vista Home Video, MGM Studios (recently sold to Sony Corporation)

Magazine and Newspapers: Five magazine publishing groups and four daily newspapers

Recreation Parks: Disneyland and twenty-seven Hotels and Disney Cruise Lines

BERTELSMANN

Television: Owns television stations and newspapers in a host of countries

Books: Bertelsmann is the world's largest publisher of books, including Random House and much more.

.

VIACOM

Television: CBS Television and Radio

Books: Publishes over two thousand times annually under thirty-eight trade names, including Simon Schuster and Scribner

Movies: Paramount Pictures

Video: Blockbuster, the world's largest renter of videos

NEWS CORPORATION
Television: Fox Television, the largest in the U.S. with twenty-one networks
Books: Harper Collins and many others
Newspapers: The *New York Post* among others
News Corporation is owned and run by right-wing Robert Murdoch

VIVENDI UNIVERSAL
Books: Sixty publishing houses that collectively sell 80 million books a year
Vivendi Telecom

GENERAL ELECTRIC
Television: NBC TV and Radio, CNBC, MSNBC, Bravo, USA
Movies: Universal Pictures
GE Aircraft Engines
GE Consumer Products
GE Industrial System
GE Power Stations
GE Transportation System

Global Inequality

The statistics collected by the United Nations are truly staggering:

- Number of people living in poverty on roughly $2 a day: 2.7 billion
- Number of people living in abject poverty existing on less than $1 a day: 1.2 billion so poor they live in garbage dumps and shantytowns, virtually without hope. Not surprisingly, 70 percent of the

world's poor are the most defenseless: women and children.

- Number of people who die every day from hunger: 24,000
- Number of children under five who die every day from preventable causes: 30,000
- 2.4 billion people live without decent sanitation, and 4 billion are without wastewater disposal.
- 275 million children never attend or complete primary school education

The 1998 Human Development Report revealed that just over 200 billionaires had a combined wealth equal to the annual incomes of just under half the global population (2.7 billion). The report found that the combined wealth of the world's three richest people was greater than the total income of the poorest forty-eight nations.

Other UN figures show that only 20 percent of the world's people have over 80 percent of the wealth and consume over 80 percent of the world's resources. This inequality is the source of ongoing violence and war, and it will only get worse until alleviated.

Or perhaps the situation is truly as dire as academician Bernard Poirot-Delpech wrote in the French newspaper *Le Monde* a few years ago: "The temptation is to shut ourselves off, cover our eyes and applaud the use of force, but the tide of the poor keeps coming, wave after wave, each time stronger and stronger. The Third World War has begun, waged by the rich against all others."

A Global Wealth Tax

Leveling a tax on international financial transactions has been proposed for years. The most popular plan to date is called the Tobin tax. Dr. James Tobin, a Nobel Laureate economist at Yale University, initiated the idea, which has been refined by later economists. It consists of a simple sales tax on currency trades across borders. Each trade on the international market, which totals nearly $2 trillion every day, would be taxed at 0.1 to 0.25 percent of volume, amounting to about twenty-five cents for every hundred dollars. This is a relatively tiny tax, but it would have a great impact on providing funds to programs designed to eradicate poverty, disease, and hunger. There has been support from several nations for this tax, but the plan needs a groundswell of support from people in rich countries like ours.

What about Globalization?

Globalization should mean movement toward a global community. The problem is that the corporate world has co-opted this term and uses it as a means to serve the multinationals and political/economic policies that make the rich even richer. Corporate globalization is unjust, undemocratic, self-destructive, and an environmental nightmare due to its dependency on mass consumption and waste.

We need new economic models that are not based on arcane and failed dogmas or those that rape the environment for profit and turn our planet into a giant marketplace where profit is all-important and there exists a deep division between rich and poor. In short, we need globalization that is democratic and serves all people of the world, and where it would be unthinkable for a few hundred billionaires to possess as much wealth as over a billion poor people.

The Environment

"Only when the last river has been poisoned, the last tree cut, the last fish caught, will man realize that he cannot eat money." This is a rough translation from Spanish that was printed a T-shirt worn by a hiker we met on a trail through the Brazilian rain forest near Iguazu Falls, and it just about sums up the environmental problems we face today.

There is such an abundance of material regarding the state of the environment and so many great organizations and people working to resolve the surrounding issues that I won't devote much time to this burning problem. The United Nations Environmental Department (UNEP) is a great source for information on the environment, and so is the Worldwatch Institute, among other organizations working to create a sustainable environment for future generations.

One specific issue that is not getting enough exposure is the danger posed by radioactive material left over from the production of nuclear weapons and energy in nuclear plants. If ever there were a crime passed on to future generations, this is it.

One of the key elements in nuclear bomb production is plutonium 239. This is a very unstable, dangerous element, a substance that, if inhaled, can be carcinogenic, with lethal consequences. It is also a danger if ingested through food or water, and it would be catastrophic if a large quantity were leaked into the soil or groundwater or released in the air.

And it gets worse. This element seemingly lasts forever. Not quite, of course, but any given amount of plutonium 239 will remain radioactive for twenty-four thousand years. It's called the element's "half-life," and it means that half of the remaining amount will be radioactive for another twenty-four thousand years, and then the remaining half of that amount for another twenty-four thousand years, and so on for hundreds of thousands of years. Other radioactive materials have a half-life ranging from seconds to minutes to days and on to over one hundred thousand years.

The government's plan for storing this material and keeping it out of danger is to place the $58 billion nuclear waste repository at Yucca Mountain, which is located one hundred miles northwest of Las Vegas. The U.S. Department of Energy wants to use the mountain to bury seventy-seven thousand tons of radioactive waste and guarantee that it will not leak or escape for at least ten thousand years.

And it gets worse! This radioactive material is currently located at nuclear power plants and nuclear weapons facilities across the country. Under the government's plan, most of this dangerous radioactive material will be transported to the Yucca Mountain repository on the nation's highways and rail lines. Not surprisingly, there are many lawsuits and a great deal of opposition to the plan for Yucca Mountain. The alternate suggestion is to leave the radioactive material where it is until a better plan can be formulated. Several plans to dispose of this material have been tentatively formed, but none is satisfying to both sides of the argument. The greater problem is that some of this dangerous material is leaking from containers at several sites and could eventually seep into the surrounding soil and groundwater; thus, a rapid resolution is critical.

A World of Mass Consumers

"The State of the World 2004" report by the Worldwatch Institute states that the world is consuming goods and services at an unsustainable pace, with serious consequences for the well-being of people and the planet itself. The report states that about 1.7 billion people worldwide—more than a quarter of humanity—have entered the "consumer class," adopting the diets, transportation systems, and lifestyles that were limited to the rich nations of Europe, North America, and Japan during most of the last century. In China alone, 240 million people have joined the ranks of consumers—a number that will soon surpass that of the United States. And further, "This rising consumption in the U.S., other rich nations, and many developing ones is more than the planet can bear."

"State of the World 2004" outlines opportunities that are already available to governments, businesses, and consumers to curb and redirect consumption: "In the long run, meeting basic human needs, improving human health, and supporting a natural world that can sustain us will require that we control consumption, rather than allow consumption to control us." However, global spending on advertising reached $446 billion in 2002, mostly aimed at convincing people to consume more and more, including cars, with the worldwide passenger car total exceeding 531 million and growing annually.

Environmentally Sustainable Economic Development, written by Nobel Laureates Trygve Haavelmo and Jan Tinbergen and World Bank economists Robert Goodland and Herman Daly, states that it is no longer reasonable to make economic growth the unquestionable objective of economic development policy. The authors contend that the world economy has already exceeded the sustainability of the global ecosystem. They maintain that it is up to rich countries to take the lead in reducing pollution and creating new avenues of growth without waste and resource depletion. Markets will have to learn to function without expansion, without wars, without waste, and without advertising that encourages waste.

New Political Leadership

Better political leadership is clearly needed across the world community, and this includes the United States. The irony is that we have an abundance of highly intelligent and capable people. The problem is convincing them to run for political office. But this problem must be overcome if we are to place individuals of wisdom in office. It is the only way to end the folly that is driving our nation backwards at an astonishing rate.

The kind of leadership we need was eloquently described by Senator William Fullbright in his book *The Price of Power*: "The age of warrior kings and of warrior presidents has passed. The nuclear age calls for a different kind of leadership—a leadership of intellect, judgment, tolerance and rationality, a leadership committed to human values, to world peace, and to the improvement of the human condition…The attributes upon which we must draw are the human attributes of compassion and understanding between cultures."

Individuals of this quality running for political office would draw legions of people, particularly young people, to work for their election with great hope and enthusiasm. This must take high priority, for a major component of the equation to build a better society and safer world is electing this quality of leadership to office.

Values and Technology

Rising in conjunction with the power of the state has been the phenomenon of modern technology that has changed human life more in the past one hundred years than in all of previous history. The vast majority of this technology has been extraordinarily beneficial to humanity, providing a better, healthier, and more comfortable life, in addition to a wealth of knowledge that people living in previous times could never have imagined. But there is another side to modern technology. It has been misused, often for profit at the expense of our life-giving environment, and even worse, to create and manufacture weapons so powerful they could end civilization.

One of the pioneers in the examination of modern technology's effect on human values was Louis Mumford. What Mumford feared was that society could become a sort of mirror image of the new machine, or what he described as the "Megamachine" in which people would be regarded as components that work solely to keep the machine running and to increase its power. There is basis to this concept when we examine the power of multinational corporations that move from country to country to employ cheaper labor. In this context, the workers receive low pay, no benefits, often terrible working conditions, and they are eventually discarded like used parts when the corporate machine moves to a new region where labor is cheaper.

In this country we have a different version called "corporate downsizing," which means that fewer people have to carry a larger load of the work, involving longer working hours and more time away from home and family. In addition, the extreme cost of living usually requires that both parents work, resulting in a more hectic life with all the other pressures and demands, especially when they have children. Even transporting to and from work on overcrowded highways has become a heavy burden for many people resulting in an extremely long workday.

Perhaps the high rate of drug use and other forms of escapism—exaggerated celebrity worship, the extreme violence in movies, television, and other forms of entertainment—can be at least partially traced to the pressure that working people face in today's society of high technology, which is often dehumanizing. And we can add to this burden the astronomical debt that most families are forced to endure because of the extreme cost of housing, medical care, school, insurance, and other essentials.

Adequate leisure time and relief from overwhelming debt is essential for a healthy and progressive society.

The Road Ahead

At this decisive moment in history, with the danger posed by a rapid proliferation of nuclear weapon states, we must act together to move the fools, the dictators, the dreamers of empire, the militarists, the arms merchants and their architects of destruction to the sideline of history. We can no long afford their destructive folly. Our unyielding task is to build a world community that respects law and justice, the sharing of resources, and the creation of a new civilization based on respect for life, respect for the environment, and respect for each other.

It can be done within a reasonable amount of time if we have the will. There are precedents for such dramatic change, such as the rise of civilization in both the Eastern and the Western world some five thousand years ago, the development of philosophical thought in the sixth century B.C. in Greece, and the rebirth of Western Civilization around the tenth century A.D.

This great advance requires that people think and act as responsible Citizens of the World. It also requires that the world's great religions perform a key role in the transformation. Nothing is more absurd than the pitting of one religion against another or murder in the name of religion. All religions share the common belief in a higher being and endow life with profound meaning. Moreover, the Golden Rule, which is a wonderful basis for human behavior, is common to all the major religions:

Judaism: What is hateful to you, do not to your fellow man. That is the entire law; all the rest is commentary.
—Talmud, Shabbat 31a—thirteenth century B.C.

Confucianism: Surely it is the maxim of loving kindness: Do not do unto others what you would not have them do unto you.
—Analects 15:23—sixth century B.C.

Buddhism: Hurt not others in ways that you yourself would find hurtful.
—Udana-Varga 5:18—fifth century B.C.

Jainism: In happiness and suffering, in joy and grief, we should regard all creatures as we regard our own self, and should therefore refrain inflicting on others such injury as would appear undesirable to us if inflicted upon ourselves.
—fifth century B.C.

Zoroastrianism: That nature alone is good which refrains from doing unto another whatsoever is not good for itself.

—Dadistan-I-dinik 94:5—fifth century B.C.

Taoism: Regard your neighbor's gain as your own gain and your neighbor's loss as your own loss.
—T'ai Shang Kan Ying P'ien—fourth century B.C.

Hinduism: This is the sum of duty: Do naught unto others which would cause you pain if done to you.
—Mahabharata 5:1517—third century B.C.

Christianity: So in everything, do to others what you would have them do to you, for this sums up the Law and the Prophets.
—Matthew 7:12—first century A.D.

Islam: No one of you is a believer until he desires for his brother that which he desires for himself.
—Sunnah—seventh century A.D.

Sikhism: Treat others as you would be treated yourself.
—sixteenth century A.D.

Beyond Here and There

There are more things in heaven and earth, Horatio, than are dreamt of in your philosophy.
—Shakespeare

Some of the new cosmological theories of the universe—how it started, where it is going, et cetera—go beyond the four dimensional universe that we have come to know and experience. New cosmologies, like the String Theory, conceive as many as ten or more dimensions to reality beyond our ability to perceive them. Perhaps overlooked is the possibility of a spiritual dimension that is the basis of all religion and that can be experienced not physically, but through faith.

In this age of high technology, new religious concepts are needed, as the famous astronomer Carl Sagan states: "A religion that stressed the magnificence of the universe as revealed by modern science, might be able to draw forth reserves of reverence and awe hardly tapped by traditional faiths. Sooner or later, such a religion will emerge."

The Bigger Picture

There's a great old song with the lyrics, "We'll meet again, don't know how, don't know when…"

Little did the composer know that it is certain that in the very distant future we will meet again, if only as scattered atoms and molecules, and we know not only how and when, but where. It's at the Great Attractor, a vast mysterious place in the distant universe about 250 million light years from our planet. Through powerful telescopes, we can view the light that left the Great Attractor 250 million years ago and is only now reaching our planet, even as it has traveled 186,000 miles per second to get here. The real nature of the Great Attractor is not understood, but its incredible gravitational pull is known and measured. Astronomers know that the Great Attractor is pulling our planet and solar system toward itself along with our entire galaxy at a rate of about 1 million miles per hour. And we are not alone: the Great Attractor is also pulling in a myriad of other galaxies in our region of the universe.

There is no escape. Whatever is left of us and our planet will arrive at the Great Attractor, but this will not occur for billions of years. So Shakespeare was right; there are far more mysteries in the real world than we can ever grasp.

On the Edge of a Galaxy

Our planet Earth orbits a star we call the sun, which is only one of 100 billion stars in the Milky Way Galaxy, and there are billions of other galaxies. Earth and the other eight planets that comprise our solar system are traveling at great speed within the mostly empty expanse of space. And yet this is the only known home of intelligent life. No other intelligent species has contacted our small planet, even though some cosmologists believe that intelligent life is not uncommon and that other intelligent species might be millions of years in advance of us. Still, there has been no contact from other intelligent species, and it's possible that none exist. At any rate, we seem to be extraordinarily rare in an incomprehensibly huge expanse of space. It is possible that we are unique within this galaxy and this universe. We have an overwhelming duty to survive and grow and to provide a future for millennia of generations to come.

And this brings us to the whole issue of human intelligence. We must never diminish the phenomenon of intelligence. Yes, condemn it when it commits barbarous acts and punish it when guilty of wrongdoing, but savor and understand just how wondrous it truly is. One way to focus on this is to take a walk for a few blocks in the downtown area of any city and make a list of what you see.

Your list will include buildings made of steel, concrete, wood, glass, and paint, and inside you will find all kinds of fabrics in the chairs, tables, and sofas, as well as electric lighting and so on. On the street you will see automobiles of all types, buses, perhaps trolley cars, and you may feel vibrations of an underground subway. In addition you will see all kinds of stores and restaurants and people dressed in an amazing variety of fabrics and designs.

There is much more to put on your list, and when you have finished you may think that your list is just a group of things. But what you have actually seen on your short journey, everywhere you looked and every object you saw, was intelligence. Every physical item was a product of human intelligence. A very short time ago, in geological terms, the same area of the city was just trees, vegetation, rocks, and soil.

But from this landscape the human mind extracted materials, from above and below the surface, from trees and vegetation, and with tremendous skill produced everything that makes up a city, from the buildings and everything in them to the sidewalks you traveled on your journey. It took millennia to acquire this store of creative knowledge, although a great deal of it, particularly the more complex aspects such as telecommunications and transportation, came within the last one hundred years.

The purpose of your walk through the city was to experience the creativity of the human mind, and perhaps this is the most amazing phenomenon in the universe—an intelligence that is aware of its own existence and acts on it, and to an amazing degree, acts knowingly upon the universe itself. We cannot waste this gift or continue to misuse it in the brutal folly of war and violence or environmental ruin. We must continue to utilize the best, the most noble of this great intelligence to accumulate more knowledge and greater understanding of our place in the vast scheme of things, and, not least, better treatment and respect for each other and respect for life itself.

What is most clear to me, with due respect to the many scientific theories to the contrary, is that this wondrous intelligence did not spring from nothingness. We are not alone.

APPENDIX
The United Nations

The History

January of 1942, representatives of twenty-six Allied nations fighting against Nazi Germany and Imperial Japan met in Washington, D.C. to support and sign the "Declaration of the United Nations."

A series of international conferences involving the U.S., United Kingdom, Soviet Union, and China were held in Moscow and Teheran, and later at Dumbarton Oaks in Washington D.C., that moved the plan for the UN closer to reality. And then at Yalta on February 11, 1945, President Roosevelt, Prime Minister Churchill, and Premier Joseph Stalin declared their resolve to establish "a general international organization to maintain peace and security." This constituted the authority to move forward to create the UN. On April 25, 1945, delegates of fifty nations met in San Francisco and created the UN Charter, which was adopted unanimously on June 25 in the San Francisco Opera House. The First General Assembly, with fifty-one nations represented, opened in Central Hall, Westminster, London on

January 10, 1946. On January 17 the Security Council met for the first time in London, adopting its rules of procedure.

On January 24, 1946, the General Assembly adopted its first resolution focusing on the peaceful uses of atomic energy and the elimination of atomic and other weapons of mass destruction.

On December 10, 1948, the General Assembly adopted the Universal Declaration of Human Rights, and on October 24, 1949, the cornerstone was laid for the present United Nations Headquarters in New York City.

On June 27, 1950, the Security Council called on Member States to help the South Korea repel invasion from the North. The Soviet Union was absent for the vote.

In 1965, UNICEF was awarded the Nobel Peace Prize.

On November 22, 1967, the Security Council adopted resolution 242 as the basis for achieving peace in the Middle East.

On June 12, 1968, the General Assembly approved the Treaty on Non-Proliferation of Nuclear Weapons and called for its ratification.

In 1969, The International Labor Organization (ILO) was awarded the Nobel Peace Prize.

On October 25, 1971, the General Assembly voted to seat representatives of the People's Republic of China.

In June of 1972, the first UN Environment Conference was held in Stockholm, Sweden, establishing the UN Environment Programme (UNEP).

In June of 1978, the General Assembly convened a special session, for the first time, on disarmament.

On May 8, 1980, three years after the last case was reported, the World Health Organization (WHO) officially declared smallpox eradicated.

In 1981, the UN High Commissioner for Refugees was awarded the Nobel Peace Prize for the second time.

On December 10, 1982, the UN Convention on the Law of the Sea was signed by one hundred seventeen States and two entities. This was the largest number of signatures ever affixed to a treaty on its first day. The United States has not ratified this treaty.

In September of 1987, the Treaty on the Protection of the Ozone Layer, known as the Montreal Protocol, was signed.

In 1988, the UN Peacekeeping operation was awarded the Nobel Peace Prize.

In June of 1992, the UN Conference on Environment and Development, the "Earth Summit," was held in Rio de Janeiro and attended by leaders from over one hundred countries. This was the largest intergovernmental gathering in history, resulting in Agenda 21, a plan of action for sustainable development.

In March of 1995, the World Summit for Social Development, one of the largest gatherings of world leaders in history, met in Copenhagen to renew the commitment to combat poverty, unemployment, and social exclusion.

On June 26, 1995, a conference was held in San Francisco, California to celebrate the fiftieth anniversary of the signing of the United Nations Charter.

On September 10, 1996, the General Assembly adopted the Comprehensive Nuclear Test-Ban Treaty. This was a turning point in the history of efforts toward nuclear disarmament and non-proliferation. The treaty was opened for signature on September 24 and has not been ratified by the United States.

On August 26, 2002, the UN World Summit on Sustainable Development was held in Johannesburg, South

Africa. This conference was attended by tens of thousands of participants, including heads of State, national delegates, and non-government organizations (NGOs).

On September 13, 2005, the UN will hold a world summit of heads of state to review progress on meeting the Millennium Development Goals.

Accomplishments

One of the silliest comments by the uninformed is that the United Nations hasn't accomplished anything important. Below is a selected list of accomplishments over the years. The full list can be viewed on the UN website at www.UN.org.

The United Nations was established in the aftermath of a devastating war to help stabilize international relations and give peace a more secure foundation. Amid the threat of nuclear war and seemingly endless regional conflicts, peacekeeping has become the overriding concern of the United Nations. In the process, the activities of blue-helmeted peacekeepers have emerged as the most visible aspect of the organization. The United Nations, however, is much more than a peacekeeper and a forum for conflict resolution. Often without attracting attention, the United Nations and its family of agencies are engaged in a vast array of work that touches every aspect of people's lives around the world:

Child survival and development. Environmental protection. Human rights. Health and medical research. Alleviation of poverty and economic development. Agricultural development and fisheries. Education. Family planning. Emergency and disaster relief. Air and sea travel. Peaceful uses of atomic energy. Labor and workers' rights.

The list goes on. Here is a sampling of what the United Nations organizations have accomplished since their founding.

1. Maintaining peace and security—By having deployed a total of fifty-four peacekeeping forces and observer missions as of September 2001, the United Nations has been able to restore calm to allow the negotiating process to go forward while saving millions of people from becoming casualties of conflicts. There are presently fifteen active peacekeeping forces in operation.

2. Making peace—Since 1945, the United Nations has been credited with negotiating many peaceful settlements that have ended regional conflicts. Recent cases include an end to the Iran-Iraq war, the withdrawal of Soviet troops from Afghanistan, and an end to the civil war in El Salvador. The United Nations has used quiet diplomacy to avert imminent wars.

3. Promoting development—The UN system has devoted more attention and resources to the promotion of the development of human skills and potentials than any other external assistance effort. The system's annual disbursements, including loans and grants, amount to more than $10 billion. The UN Development Programme (UNDP), in close cooperation with over 170 Member States and other UN agencies, designs and implements projects for agriculture, industry, education, and the environment.

4. Promoting human rights—Since adopting the Universal Declaration of Human Rights in 1948, the United Nations has helped enact dozens of comprehensive agreements on political, civil, economic, social, and cultural rights.

5. Protecting the environment—The United Nations has played a vital role in fashioning a global program designed to protect the environment. The "Earth Summit," the UN Conference on Environment and Development held in Rio de Janeiro in 1992, resulted in treaties on biodiversity and climate change, and all countries adopted "Agenda 21"—a blueprint to promote sustainable development or the concept of economic growth while protecting natural resources.

6. Preventing nuclear proliferation—The United Nations, through the International Atomic Energy Agency, has helped minimize the threat of a nuclear war by inspecting nuclear reactors in ninety countries to ensure that nuclear materials are not diverted for military purposes.

7. Strengthening international law—Over three hundred international treaties, on topics as varied as human rights conventions to agreements on the use of outer space and seabed, have been enacted through the efforts of the United Nations.

8. Ending apartheid in South Africa—By imposing measures ranging from an arms embargo to a

convention against segregated sporting events, the United Nations was a major factor in bringing about the downfall of the apartheid system, which the General Assembly called "a crime against humanity."

9. Providing humanitarian aid to victims of conflict—More than 30 million refugees fleeing war, famine, or persecution have received aid from the UN High Commissioner for Refugees since 1951 in a continuing effort coordinated by the United Nations that often involves other agencies. There are more than 19 million refugees, mostly women and children, who are receiving food, shelter, medical aid, education, and repatriation assistance.

10. Alleviating chronic hunger and rural poverty in developing countries—The International Fund for Agricultural Development (IFAD) has developed a system of providing credit, often in very small amounts, for the poorest and most marginalized groups that has benefited over 230 million people in nearly one hundred developing countries.

11. Promoting women's rights—A long-term objective of the United Nations has been to improve the lives of women and to empower women to have greater control over their lives. Several conferences during the UN-sponsored International Women's Decade set an agenda for the advancement of women and women's rights for the rest of the century. The UN Development Fund for Women (UNIFEM) and the International Research and Training Institute for the

Advancement of Women (INSTRAW) have supported programs and projects to improve the quality of life for women in over one hundred countries.

12. Providing safe drinking water—UN agencies have worked to make safe drinking water available to 1.3 billion people in rural areas during the last decade.

13. Eradicating smallpox—A thirteen-year effort by the World Health Organization resulted in the complete eradication of smallpox from the planet in 1980. WHO also helped wipe out polio from the Western hemisphere.

14. Pressing for universal immunization—Polio, tetanus, measles, whooping cough, diphtheria, and tuberculosis still kill more than 8 million children each year. In 1974, only 5 percent of children in developing countries were immunized against these diseases. Today, as a result of the efforts of UNICEF and WHO, there is an 80 percent immunization rate, saving the lives of more than 3 million children each year.

15. Reducing child mortality rates—Through oral rehydration therapy, water sanitation, and other health and nutrition measures undertaken by UN agencies, child mortality rates in the developing countries have been halved since 1960, increasing the life expectancy from thirty-seven to sixty-seven years.

16. Reducing the effects of natural disasters—The World Meteorological Organization (WMO) has spared millions of people from the calamitous effects of both natural and man-made disasters. Its early warning system, which utilizes thousands of surface monitors as well as satellites, has provided information for the dispersal of oil spills and has predicted long-term droughts.

17. Providing food to victims of emergencies—Nearly 815 million people are currently suffering from chronic malnutrition, including 300 million children. In 2001, the World Food Programme (WFP) distributed 4.2 million tons of food to 77 million people in eighty-two countries for a total operational expenditure of $1.74 billion. Twenty million people received, through development projects, aid in food-for-work projects to promote agriculture and improve the environment, and in school feeding, health, and nutrition projects. Fifty-seven million people were offered assistance through short- and long-term operations.

18. Clearing land mines—The United Nations is leading an international effort to clear land mines from former battlefields in Afghanistan, Angola, Cambodia, El Salvador, Mozambique, Rwanda, and Somalia that still kill and maim thousands of innocent people every year.

19. Preventing over-fishing—The Food and Agriculture Organization (FAO) monitors marine fishery

production and issues alerts to prevent damage due to over-fishing.

20. Limiting deforestation and promoting sustainable forestry development—FAO, UNDP, and the World Bank, through a Tropical Forests Action Programme, have formulated and carried out forestry action plans in ninety countries.

21. Cleaning up pollution—UNEP led a major effort to clean up the Mediterranean Sea. It encouraged adversaries such as Syria and Israel, Turkey and Greece to work together to clean up beaches. As a result, more than 50 percent of the previously polluted beaches are now usable.

22. Reducing fertility rates—The UN Population Fund (UNFPA), through its family planning programs, has enabled people to make informed choices, and consequently given families, and especially women, greater control over their lives. As a result, women in developing countries are having fewer children— from 6 births per woman in the 1960s to 3.5 today. In the 1960s, only 10 percent of the world's families were using effective methods of family planning. The number now stands at 55 percent.

23. Promoting economic reform—Together with the World Bank and the International Monetary Fund, the United Nations has helped many countries improve their economic management, offered training for government finance officials, and provided

financial assistance to countries experiencing temporary balance of payment difficulties.

24. Promoting worker rights—The International Labor Organization (ILO) has worked to guarantee freedom of the right to association, the right to organize, collective bargaining, the rights of indigenous and tribal peoples; has promoted employment and equal remuneration; and has sought to eliminate discrimination and child labor.

25. Promoting stability and order in the world's oceans— Through three international conferences, the third lasting more than nine years, the United Nations has spearheaded an international effort to promote a comprehensive global agreement for the protection, preservation, and peaceful development of the oceans. The UN Convention on the Law of the Sea, which came into force in 1994, lays down rules for the determination of national maritime jurisdiction, navigation on the high seas, rights and duties of coastal and other states, obligation to protect and preserve the marine environment, cooperation in the conduct of marine scientific research, and preservation of living resources.

26. Improving air and sea travel—UN agencies have been responsible for setting safety standards for sea and air travel. The efforts of the International Civil Aviation Organization (ICAO) have contributed to making air travel the safest mode of transportation. To wit: In 1947, when 9 million traveled, 590 were killed in

aircraft accidents; in 1993, the number of deaths was
936 out of the 1.2 billion airline passengers. Over the
last two decades, pollution from tankers has been
reduced by as much as 60 percent thanks to the work
of the International Maritime Organization (IMO).

27. Improving global communications—The Universal
    Postal Union (UPU) has maintained and regulated
    international mail delivery. The International
    Telecommunications Union (ITU) has coordinated
    use of the radio spectrum, promoted cooperation in
    assigning positions for stationary satellites, and
    established international standards for
    communications, thereby ensuring the unfettered
    flow of information around the globe.

28. Establishing "children as a zone of peace"—From El
    Sudan to former Yugoslavia, UNICEF pioneered the
    establishment of "Days of Tranquility" and the
    opening of "Corridors of Peace" to provide vaccines
    and other assistance desperately needed by children
    caught in armed conflict.

29. Improving education in developing countries—As a
    direct result of the efforts of UN agencies, over 60
    percent of adults in developing countries can now
    read and write, and 90 percent of children in these
    countries attend school.

30. Improving literacy for women—Programs aimed at
    promoting education and advancement for women
    helped raise steadily the female literacy rate in

developing countries from 36 percent in 1970 to 56 percent in 1990 and to 72 percent in 2000.

31. Safeguarding and preserving historic cultural and architectural sites—Ancient monuments in eighty-one countries including Greece, Egypt, Italy, Indonesia, and Cambodia, have been protected through the efforts of UNESCO, and international conventions have been adopted to preserve cultural property.

How the UN Works

The principle organs of the United Nations are the Security Council, the General Assembly, the International Court of Justice, the Economic and Social Council, and the Secretariat. In addition there are over forty Specialized Agencies and Programs. A thumbnail description follows:

The responsibility of the **Security Council** is the maintenance of international peace and security. It is currently structured with five permanent members that have veto power over all issues brought before the council. The permanent members are the U.S., Russia, China, France, and UK. The council has ten rotating Member States to complete the fifteen total. The presidency of the Council rotates monthly.

The **General Assembly** is composed of representatives of all Member States, each of which has one vote. This is the main deliberative organ of the United Nations. Decisions of crucial issues, such as peace and security, the admission of new members, and the UN budget, require a two-thirds majority. A simple majority is required on other issues.

The **Secretariat** has an international staff working in stations around the world with the duty of carrying out the day-to-day work of the organization.

The Secretariat services all the principal organs of the United Nations and administers the programs and policies. The Secretariat is led by the Secretary General, who is appointed by the General Assembly on the recommendation of the Security Council for a five-year term. The Secretariat has a staff of roughly nine thousand international civil servants.

The **International Court of Justice** is the principle judicial organ of the United Nations and is located at the Peace Palace in The Hague (Netherlands). The court has two roles, the first of which is to settle in accordance with international law the legal disputes submitted to it by States, and the second of which is to give advisory opinions of legal questions referred to it by duly authorized international organs and agencies. The Court is composed of fifteen judges elected to nine-year terms of office by the General Assembly and Security Council, sitting independently of each other.

The **Economic and Social Council** is the principal organ to coordinate the economic, social, and related work of the UN specialized agencies, functional commissions, and five regional commissions. The Council serves as the central forum for discussing international economic and social issues, and for formulating policy recommendations addressed to Member States and the United Nations system. With its broad mandate, the Council's purview extends to over 70 percent of the human and financial resources of the entire UN system.

The **International Court of Justice** (ICC) is not part of the United Nations Organization, but it was created through the United Nations; therefore, a description of the court follows.

The ICC was established by a treaty called the Rome Statute, which entered into force on July 1, 2002. By 2004, ninety-seven countries ratified the Rome Statute and joined the ICC, including most all the democracies in the world. The ICC has the purpose of ending the cycle of impunity for the most serious crimes of international concern and will decide on the criminal responsibility of individuals and act as a deterrent for possible future criminal acts. The ICC will prosecute the worst crimes of humanity identified as Genocide, War Crimes, and Crimes Against Humanity. The ICC has eighteen judges who serve nine-year, non-renewable terms. President Clinton signed on to the International Criminal Court (ICC) on December 31, 2000. The Bush administration is totally against U.S. participation in the ICC and nullified the U.S. signature by sending a letter to UN Secretary General Kofi Annan on May 6, 2002, expressing its intention not to be bound by the treaty.

United Nations Development Program (UNDP)

The UNDP is the UN's global development network with programs in 166 countries that work with the people to achieve their development goals. UNDP publishes the annual Human Development Report that provides analysis on global issues of all Member States.

United Nations Education, Scientific and Cultural Organization (UNESCO)

UNESCO promotes international cooperation among its 192 Member States and 6 Associate Members in the fields of education, science, culture, and communication. UNESCO has trained teachers and built schools around the world. It protects our human heritage and conducts important scientific conferences.

United Nations International Children's Emergency Fund (UNICEF)

Probably the best known of all the UN's specialized agencies, UNICEF is the world's leading organization working specifically for children, working with communities and governments in 158 countries to aid children with emergency relief and long-term programs in health, education, and child protection. UNICEF'S programs have saved the lives of millions of children around the world.

United Nations High Commissioner for Refugees (UNHCR)

UNHCR leads and coordinates international action to protect refugees and resolve their problems worldwide. In the past fifty years, this agency has helped an estimated 50 million people restart their lives. UNHCR is working in over one hundred countries to help some 17 million refugees.

United Nations Fund for Population Activities (UNFPA)

UNFPA is the world's largest international organization for population and reproductive health programs, working with governments and non-government organizations in over 140 countries. The world population in 2005 is 6.4 billion and growing rapidly at 76 million persons per year. The UN estimates the world population by 2050 will be about 9 billion.

World Health Organization (WHO)

WHO is active in countries around the world in combating disease and working to attain the best possible level of health for all people in the world.

International Labor Organization (ILO)

ILO promotes social justice and internationally recognized human and labor rights, including setting minimum standards of basic labor rights, freedom of association, the right to organize, collective bargaining, abolition of forced labor, and other standards regulating conditions of work related issues.

World Meteorological Organization (WMO)

WMO has membership in 187 countries and issues over one hundred thousand weather forecasts every day all around the world, contributing substantially to the protection of life and property against natural disasters.

Universal Postal Union (UPU)

Ever wonder why you feel secure in sending mail to remote parts of the world? It's UPU that gives you comfort by working with all countries to ensure that mail is delivered, and what a gigantic task that is. UPU reports there are seven hundred thousand post offices in the world. Mail is handled by 6.2 million postal workers, and they carry over 400 billion letters every year.

There are a great many other important UN agencies that benefit people every day, including regulating and providing safety issues for civil aviation, ships at sea, and telecommunications. There is also the United Nations University, the Joint United Nations Program on HIV/AIDS

(UNAIDS), the United Nations Research Institute for Social Development (UNRISD), the United Nations Conference on Trade and Development (UNCTAD), and much more. The realty is that the UN plays an important role in our everyday life. Sadly, only a minority is aware of it.

The Fork in the Road

This is how Secretary General Kofi Annan describes the present state of the United Nations, and why he states "the 2005 Summit will be an event of decisive importance. The decisions to be taken there may determine the whole future of the United Nations."

The meeting is to review the Millennium Development Goals that were agreed by the consensus of all Member States in 2000. Below are some selected Millennium Goals of the Millennium Declaration of 2000. The full declaration can be read on the UN website.

I. Values and Principles

We, heads of State and Government, have gathered at the United Nations Headquarters in New York from 6 to 8 September 2000, at the dawn of a new millennium, to reaffirm our faith in the organization and its Charter as indispensable foundations of a more peaceful, prosperous and just world.

We are determined to establish a just and lasting peace all over the world in accordance with the purposes and principles of the Charter...

We consider certain fundamental values to be essential to international relations in the twenty-first century: Freedom—Equality—Solidarity—Tolerance—Respect for nature—Shared responsibility.

II. Peace, Security and Disarmament

We will spare no effort to free our peoples from the scourge of war, whether within or between States, which has claimed more than 5 million lives in the past decade. We will also seek to eliminate the dangers posed by weapons of mass destruction.

To make the United Nations more effective in maintaining peace and security by giving it the resources and tools it needs for conflict prevention, peaceful resolution of disputes, peacekeeping...

To strive for the elimination of weapons of mass destruction, particularly nuclear weapons, and to keep all options open for achieving this aim...

NOTE that this commitment was made more precisely in Article IV of the Non-Proliferation Treaty as follows::

"Each of the parties to the treaty undertakes to pursue negotiations in good faith on effective measures relating to cessation of the nuclear arms race at an early date and to nuclear disarmament, and on a treaty on general and complete disarmament under strict and effective international control."

III. Development and Poverty Eradication

We will spare no effort to free our fellow men, women and children from the abject and dehumanizing conditions of extreme poverty, to which more than a billion of them are currently subjected...

To implement the enhanced program of debt relief for the heavily indebted poor countries without further delay and to agree to cancel all official bilateral debts of those countries in return for their making demonstrable commitments to poverty reduction...

To halve, by the year 2015, the proportion of the world's people whose income is less than one dollar a day and the proportion of people who suffer from hunger and, at the same date, to halve the proportion of people who are unable to reach safe drinking water...

By 2020 to have achieved a significant improvement in the lives of at least 100 million slum dwellers...

IV. Protecting our Common Environment

We must spare no effort to free all humanity, and above all our children and grandchildren, from the threat of living on a planet irredeemably spoilt by human activities, and whose resources would no longer be sufficient for their needs...

V. Human Rights, Democracy and Good Governance

We will spare no effort to promote democracy and strengthen the rule of law, as well as respect for all internationally recognized human rights and fundamental freedoms...

To respect fully and uphold the Universal Declaration of Human Rights

To work collectively for more inclusive political processes, allowing genuine participation by all citizens in all our countries...

To ensure the freedom of the media to perform their essential role and the right of the public to have access to information...

VII. Meeting the Special Needs of Africa

We will support the consolidation of democracy in Africa and assist Africans in their struggle for lasting peace, poverty eradication and sustainable development, thereby bringing Africa into the mainstream of the world economy.

To help Africa build up its capacity to tackle the spread of the HIV/AIDS pandemic and other infectious diseases.

VIII. Strengthening the United Nations

We will spare no effort to make the United Nations a more effective instrument for pursuing all of these priorities: the fight for development for all the peoples of the world; the fight against poverty, ignorance and disease; the fight against injustice; the fight against violence, terror and crime; and the fight against the degradation and destruction of our common home...

We solemnly reaffirm, on this historic occasion, that the United Nations is the indispensable common house of the entire human family, through which we will seek to realize our universal aspirations for peace, cooperation and development. We therefore pledge our unstinting support for these common objectives and our determination to achieve them.

On December 10, 1948, the General Assembly of the United Nations adopted and proclaimed the Universal Declaration of Human Rights. This is one of the great milestones in human history. The full text follows:

PREAMBLE

Whereas recognition of the inherent dignity and of the equal and inalienable rights of all members of the human family is the foundation of freedom, justice and peace in the world,

Whereas disregard and contempt for human rights have resulted in barbarous acts which have outraged the conscience of mankind, and the advent of a world in which human beings shall enjoy freedom of speech and belief and freedom from fear and want has been proclaimed as the highest aspiration of the common people,

Whereas it is essential, if man is not to be compelled to have recourse, as a last resort, to rebellion against tyranny and oppression, that human rights should be protected by the rule of law,

Whereas it is essential to promote the development of friendly relations between nations,

Whereas the peoples of the United Nations have in the Charter reaffirmed their faith in fundamental human rights, in the dignity and worth of the human person and in the equal rights of men and women and have determined to promote social progress and better standards of life in larger freedom,

Whereas Member States have pledged themselves to achieve, in co-operation with the United Nations, the promotion of universal respect for and observance of human rights and fundamental freedoms,

Whereas a common understanding of these rights and freedoms is of the greatest importance for the full realization of this pledge,

Now, Therefore THE GENERAL ASSEMBLY proclaims THIS UNIVERSAL DECLARATION OF HUMAN RIGHTS as a common standard of achievement for all peoples and all nations, to the end that every individual and every organ of society, keeping this Declaration constantly in mind, shall strive by teaching and education to promote respect for these rights and freedoms and by progressive measures, national and international, to secure their universal and effective recognition and observance, both among the peoples of

Member States themselves and among the peoples of territories under their jurisdiction.

Article 1. All human beings are born free and equal in dignity and rights. They are endowed with reason and conscience and should act towards one another in a spirit of brotherhood.

Article 2. Everyone is entitled to all the rights and freedoms set forth in this Declaration, without distinction of any kind, such as race, colour, sex, language, religion, political or other opinion, national or social origin, property, birth or other status. Furthermore, no distinction shall be made on the basis of the political, jurisdictional or international status of the country or territory to which a person belongs, whether it be independent, trust, non-self-governing or under any other limitation of sovereignty.

Article 3. Everyone has the right to life, liberty and security of person.

Article 4. No one shall be held in slavery or servitude; slavery and the slave trade shall be prohibited in all their forms.

Article 5. No one shall be subjected to torture or to cruel, inhuman or degrading treatment or punishment.

Article 6. Everyone has the right to recognition everywhere as a person before the law.

Article 7. All are equal before the law and are entitled without any discrimination to equal protection of the law. All are entitled to equal protection against any discrimination in violation of this Declaration and against any incitement to such discrimination.

Article 8. Everyone has the right to an effective remedy by the competent national tribunals for acts violating the fundamental rights granted him by the constitution or by law.

Article 9. No one shall be subjected to arbitrary arrest, detention or exile.

Article 10. Everyone is entitled in full equality to a fair and public hearing by an independent and impartial tribunal, in the determination of his rights and obligations and of any criminal charge against him.

Article 11.

(1) Everyone charged with a penal offence has the right to be presumed innocent until proved guilty according to law in a public trial at which he has had all the guarantees necessary for his defence.

(2) No one shall be held guilty of any penal offence on account of any act or omission which did not constitute a penal offence, under national or international law, at the time when it was committed. Nor shall a heavier penalty be imposed than the one that was applicable at the time the penal offence was committed.

Article 12. No one shall be subjected to arbitrary interference with his privacy, family, home or correspondence, nor to attacks upon his honour and reputation. Everyone has the right to the protection of the law against such interference or attacks.

Article 13.

(1) Everyone has the right to freedom of movement and residence within the borders of each state.

(2) Everyone has the right to leave any country, including his own, and to return to his country.

Article 14.

(1) Everyone has the right to seek and to enjoy in other countries asylum from persecution.

(2) This right may not be invoked in the case of prosecutions genuinely arising from non-political crimes or from acts contrary to the purposes and principles of the United Nations.

Article 15.

(1) Everyone has the right to a nationality.

(2) No one shall be arbitrarily deprived of his nationality nor denied the right to change his nationality.

Article 16.

(1) Men and women of full age, without any limitation due to race, nationality or religion, have the right to marry and to found a family. They are entitled to equal rights as to marriage, during marriage and at its dissolution.

(2) Marriage shall be entered into only with the free and full consent of the intending spouses.

(3) The family is the natural and fundamental group unit of society and is entitled to protection by society and the State.

Article 17.

(1) Everyone has the right to own property alone as well as in association with others.

(2) No one shall be arbitrarily deprived of his property.

Article 18. Everyone has the right to freedom of thought, conscience and religion; this right includes freedom to change his religion or belief, and freedom, either alone or in community with others and in public or private, to manifest his religion or belief in teaching, practice, worship and observance.

Article 19. Everyone has the right to freedom of opinion and expression; this right includes freedom to hold opinions without interference and to seek, receive and impart information and ideas through any media and regardless of frontiers.

Article 20.

(1) Everyone has the right to freedom of peaceful assembly and association.

(2) No one may be compelled to belong to an association.

Article 21.

(1) Everyone has the right to take part in the government of his country, directly or through freely chosen representatives.

(2) Everyone has the right of equal access to public service in his country.

(3) The will of the people shall be the basis of the authority of government; this will shall be expressed in periodic and genuine elections which shall be by universal and equal suffrage and shall be held by secret vote or by equivalent free voting procedures.

Article 22. Everyone, as a member of society, has the right to social security and is entitled to realization, through national effort and international co-operation and in accordance with the organization and resources of each State, of the economic, social and cultural rights indispensable for his dignity and the free development of his personality.

Article 23

(1) Everyone has the right to work, to free choice of employment, to just and favourable conditions of work and to protection against unemployment.

(2) Everyone, without any discrimination, has the right to equal pay for equal work.

(3) Everyone who works has the right to just and favourable remuneration ensuring for himself and his family an existence worthy of human dignity, and supplemented, if necessary, by other means of social protection.

(4) Everyone has the right to form and to join trade unions for the protection of his interests.

Article 24. Everyone has the right to rest and leisure, including reasonable limitation of working hours and periodic holidays with pay.

Article 25.

(1) Everyone has the right to a standard of living adequate for the health and well-being of himself and of his family, including food, clothing, housing and medical care and necessary social services, and the right to security in the event of unemployment, sickness, disability, widowhood, old age or other lack of livelihood in circumstances beyond his control.

(2) Motherhood and childhood are entitled to special care and assistance. All children, whether born in or out of wedlock, shall enjoy the same social protection.

Article 26.

(1) Everyone has the right to education. Education shall be free, at least in the elementary and fundamental stages. Elementary education shall be compulsory. Technical and professional education shall be made generally available and higher education shall be equally accessible to all on the basis of merit.

(2) Education shall be directed to the full development of the human personality and to the strengthening of respect for human rights and fundamental freedoms. It shall promote understanding, tolerance and friendship among all nations, racial or religious groups, and shall further the activities of the United Nations for the maintenance of peace.

(3) Parents have a prior right to choose the kind of education that shall be given to their children.

Article 27.

(1) Everyone has the right freely to participate in the cultural life of the community, to enjoy the arts and to share in scientific advancement and its benefits.

(2) Everyone has the right to the protection of the moral and material interests resulting from any scientific, literary or artistic production of which he is the author.

Article 28. Everyone is entitled to a social and international order in which the rights and freedoms set forth in this Declaration can be fully realized.

Article 29.

(1) Everyone has duties to the community in which alone the free and full development of his personality is possible.

(2) In the exercise of his rights and freedoms, everyone shall be subject only to such limitations as are determined by law solely for the purpose of securing due recognition and respect for the rights and freedoms of others and of meeting the just requirements of morality, public order and the general welfare in a democratic society.

(3) These rights and freedoms may in no case be exercised contrary to the purposes and principles of the United Nations.

Article 30.

Nothing in this Declaration may be interpreted as implying for any State, group or person any right to engage in any activity or to perform any act aimed at the destruction of any of the rights and freedoms set forth herein.

Covenant on Economic, Social, and Cultural Rights

This covenant describes the basic economic, social, and cultural rights of individuals and nations, including the right to:

- self-determination
- wages sufficient to support a minimum standard of living
- equal pay for equal work
- equal opportunity for advancement
- form trade unions

- strike
- paid or otherwise compensated maternity leave
- free primary education, and accessible education at all levels
- copyright, patent, and trademark protection for intellectual property

In addition, this covenant forbids exploitation of children and requires all nations to cooperate to end world hunger. Each nation that has ratified this covenant is required to submit annual reports on its progress in providing for these rights to the Secretary General, who is to transmit them to the Economic and Social Council. The text of this covenant was finalized in 1966 along with that of the Covenant on Civil and Political Rights.

UN Peacekeeping Organizations

UN peacekeeping is one of the most important UN operations, and yet one that is often belittled, misunderstood, and unknown to most Americans. In its history the UN has conducted fifty-nine peacekeeping operations, and sixteen are in operation today, keeping the peace in areas that would otherwise be engaged in war.

From the UN Website:

Peacekeeping is a way to help countries torn by conflict create conditions for sustainable peace. UN peacekeepers—soldiers and military officers, civilian police officers and civilian personnel from many countries—monitor and observe peace processes that emerge in post-conflict situations and assist ex-combatants to implement the peace agreements they have signed. Such assistance comes in many forms, including confidence-building measures, power-sharing arrangements, electoral support, strengthening the rule of law, and economic and social development.

The Charter of the United Nations gives the UN Security Council the power and responsibility to take collective action to maintain international peace and security. For this reason, the international community usually looks to the Security Council to authorize peacekeeping operations. Most of these operations are established and implemented by the United Nations itself with troops serving under UN operational command. In other cases, where direct UN involvement is not considered appropriate or feasible, the Council authorizes regional organizations such as the North Atlantic Treaty Organization, the Economic Community of West African States, or coalitions of willing countries to implement certain peacekeeping or peace enforcement functions.

Non-Government Organizations (NGOs)

If the UN's global agenda is to be properly addressed, a partnership with civil society at large is not an option, it is a necessity.
—Kofi Annan, Secretary General of the United Nations

A non-government organization (NGO) is a non-profit volunteer organization comprised of people with a common interest or purpose. Peace and human rights organizations are typical NGOs. About fourteen hundred NGOs from all regions of the world are associated with the United Nations Department of Public Information (DPI). NGOs offer analysis and expertise and help monitor international agreements, and they provide an invaluable service in educating the general public on the role and activities of the United Nations.

Over twenty-six hundred NGOs have consultative status with the United Nations Economic and Social Council (ECOSOC). This status is granted on the recommendation of the ECOSOC Committee on NGOs, which is comprised of nineteen Member States, and is based on Article 71 of the UN Charter. NGOs participate in ECOSOC through attending meetings and providing ideas on agenda items. Some NGOs are invited to attend international conferences called by the UN General Assembly and other agencies. NGOs have performed an important role in the Earth Summit.

International Meetings Organized by the UN

Many NGOs perform a vital role in UN Specialized Agencies and programs. Some NGOs are also in the forefront in working and pushing for UN reform programs and providing much needed suggestions for change. This includes attaining a larger role for NGOs at the UN, perhaps at some point to include a Peoples Parliament within the General Assembly. In 1995, former UN Secretary General Perez de Cuellar's World Commission on Culture and Development recommended that a "two-chamber General Assembly could be considered, one with government representatives as at present, and the other representing national civil society organizations." In the same year, the Commission on Global Governance proposed "an annual Forum of Civil Society (to) consist of representatives of organizations accredited to the General Assembly as Civil Society Organizations" (CSOs).

In 1995, the world governments approved the following UN Declaration:

We recognize that our common work will be more successful if it is supported by all concerned actors in the international community, including non-governmental organizations (NGOs), multilateral financial institutions, regional organizations and all actors of civil society. We will welcome and facilitate such support, as appropriate.

ACKNOWLEDGMENTS

My special thanks and acknowledgment to Connie Braveheart, Kate Christensen, and Amy Tackett for their editorial assistance.